MONTHLY PAYMENT TABLES

on

MORTGAGE LOANS

FROM 5% TO 30%
FROM $ 500 TO $ 100 000

Published by :
Transaction Financial Guides

Distribution :
Maptique Inc.
JDMG

Legal deposit :
1st quarter 1986
Quebec and Canada

ISBN : 2-89074-901-0

PRINTED IN CANADA

HOW TO USE
THE TABLES

How to use the tables:

The tables of this book show the monthly payments to be calculated to pay off a mortage loan with compound interest, according to the method used by most of the banks.

The method of calculating compound interest, is based on fixed periods, even if these periods vary between each payment.

This small guide can help you, when you want to find out the monthly amount to pay off your mortage loan.

The method of determining the monthly required payment of your mortage loan, is very simple: using the interest rate tables, look up the amount owed according to the loan term (months or years).

If you want to know how much to pay each month, for a one year mortgage loan of $ 1 000.00, at a rate of 14 %, you only have to look in the 14 % tables in the horizontal line titled "amount". When it intersects the column titled "terms of loan" (the one marked one year) you will find the application payment, which is $ 89.61.

Rates between 6 to 21% are available in 1/4%. From 5 to 6%, and 21 to 25%, they are available in 1/2%. From 25 to 30%, whole numbers only are used.

The amounts start at $500.00, and rise by thousands up to $10 000.00 by five thousands up to $50 000.00, and finally by ten thousands up to $100 000.00

To determine a monthly payment of an amount not shown in the tables, parts of amounts must be used to equate the required amount.

For example, let us take a $47 500.00 loan at a rate of 14% for a term of 20 years. You only need to add up the owed amount for $45 000.00, then for $2 000.00, and for $500.00 : which makes :

$$ \$ 546.83 + \$ 24.31 + \$ 6.08 = \$ 577.22 $$

It is the same thing for the amounts lower than the given numbers. For a multiple of 10, you only have to move the decimal point one digit to the left, which gives us :

$ 1 000. at 14% is $ 23.07 for five years
$ 100 at 14% is $ 2.31 for five years

For an amount lower than $500, as for example $320; take the amount corresponding to $3 200.00, which is a multiple of 10 above $ 500. Then move the decimal point one digit to the left (or two, as the case may be) which gives :

For $ 3 200.00 at 14 %
    — for $ 3 000 at 14 % = $ 268.81 +
    — for $ 200, we take $ 2 000 = $ 179.21
      moved to $ 17.92

So, $ 268.81 + $ 17.92 = $ 286.73 for 1 year
For $ 320 at 14 % = $ 28.67 for 1 year

MONTHLY PAYMENT TABLES

From 5% to 30%
From $ 500 to $ 100 000

5% Required monthly payment to refund a mortgage loan

Amount	terms of loan (in years)					
	1	2	3	4	5	10
500	42,80	21,93	14,98	11,51	9,43	5,30
1 000	85,59	43,85	29,95	23,01	18,85	10,59
2 000	171,17	87,70	59,90	46,02	37,70	21,17
3 000	256,76	131,55	89,85	69,02	56,55	31,74
4 000	342,34	175,40	119,80	92,02	75,40	43,33
5 000	427,92	219,24	149,74	115,03	94,24	52,91
6 000	513,51	263,09	179,69	138,06	113,09	63,49
7 000	599,09	306,94	209,64	161,05	131,94	74,07
8 000	684,68	350,79	239,59	184,05	150,79	84,65
9 000	770,26	394,64	269,54	207,06	169,64	95,23
10 000	855,84	438,40	294,48	230,06	188,48	105,81
15 000	1283,76	657,72	449,37	345,09	282,72	158,72
20 000	1711,68	876,96	598,96	460,12	376,96	211,62
25 000	2139,60	1096,20	748,70	575,15	471,20	264,53
30 000	2567,52	1315,44	898,44	690,18	565,44	317,43
35 000	2995,44	1534,68	1048,18	805,21	659,68	370,34
40 000	3423,36	1753,92	1197,92	920,24	753,92	423,24
45 000	3851,28	1973,16	1347,66	1035,27	848,16	476,15
50 000	4279,20	2192,40	1796,88	1150,30	942,40	529,05
60 000	5135,04	2630,88	1796,88	1380,36	1130,88	634,86
70 000	5990,88	3069,36	2096,36	1610,42	1319,36	740,67
80 000	6846,72	3507,84	2395,84	1840,48	1507,84	846,48
90 000	7702,56	3946,32	2695,32	2070,54	1696,32	952,29
100 000	8558,40	4384,80	2994,80	2300,60	1884,80	1058,10

Required monthly payment to refund a mortgage loan

5%

Amount	terms of loan (in years)					
	15	20	25	30	35	40
500	3,95	3,29	2,91	2,67	2,51	2,40
1 000	7,89	6,58	5,82	5,34	5,02	4,79
2 000	15,77	13,15	11,64	10,65	10,03	9,58
3 000	23,65	19,72	17,45	16,02	15,05	14,37
4 000	31,53	26,29	23,27	21,35	20,06	19,16
5 000	39,40	32,86	29,08	26,69	25,07	23,94
6 000	47,29	39,43	34,90	32,03	30,09	28,73
7 000	55,17	46,00	40,72	37,36	35,10	33,52
8 000	63,05	52,57	46,53	42,69	40,12	38,31
9 000	70,93	59,14	52,35	48,04	45,13	43,10
10 000	78,81	65,71	58,16	53,37	50,14	47,88
15 000	118,22	98,57	87,24	80,06	75,21	71,82
20 000	157,62	131,42	116,32	106,74	100,28	95,76
25 000	197,03	164,28	145,40	133,43	125,35	119,70
30 000	236,43	197,13	174,48	160,11	150,42	143,64
35 000	275,83	229,99	203,56	186,80	175,49	167,58
40 000	315,24	262,84	232,64	213,48	200,56	191,52
45 000	354,65	295,70	261,72	240,17	225,63	215,46
50 000	394,05	328,55	290,80	266,85	250,70	239,40
60 000	472,86	394,26	348,96	320,22	300,84	287,28
70 000	551,67	459,98	407,12	373,59	350,98	335,16
80 000	630,48	525,68	465,28	426,96	401,12	383,04
90 000	709,29	591,39	523,44	480,33	451,26	430,92
100 000	788,10	657,10	581,60	533,70	501,40	478,80

5½%   Required monthly payment to refund a mortgage loan

Amount	terms of loan (in years)					
	1	2	3	4	5	10
500	42,91	22,04	15,09	11,62	9,54	5,42
1 000	85,81	44,07	30,17	23,23	19,08	10,83
2 000	171,62	88,14	60,34	46,46	38,15	21,65
3 000	257,43	132,21	90,50	69,69	57,21	32,47
4 000	343,24	176,28	120,68	92,92	76,29	43,29
5 000	429,04	220,34	150,84	116,14	95,37	54,11
6 000	514,85	264,41	181,01	139,37	114,44	64,94
7 000	600,66	308,48	211,18	162,60	133,52	75,76
8 000	686,47	352,55	241,35	185,83	152,58	86,58
9 000	772,27	396,62	271,52	209,06	171,66	97,40
10 000	858,08	440,68	301,68	232,28	190,73	108,22
15 000	1287,12	661,02	452,52	348,42	286,10	162,33
20 000	1716,16	881,36	603,36	464,56	381,46	216.44
25 000	2145,20	1101,70	754,20	580,70	476,83	270,55
30 000	2574,24	1322,04	905,04	696,84	572,19	324,66
35 000	3003,28	1542,38	1055,88	812,98	667,56	378,77
40 000	3432,32	1762,72	1206,72	929,12	762,92	432,88
45 000	3861,36	1983,06	1357,56	1045,26	858,29	486,99
50 000	4290,40	2203,40	1508,40	1161,40	953,65	541,10
60 000	5148,48	2644,08	1810,08	1393,68	1144,38	649,32
70 000	6006,56	3084,76	2111,76	1625,96	1335,11	757,54
80 000	6864,64	3525,44	2413,44	1858,24	1525,84	865,76
90 000	7722,72	3966,12	2715,12	2090,52	1716,57	973,98
100 000	8580,80	4406,80	3016,80	2322,80	1907,30	1082,20

Required monthly payment to refund a mortgage loan

5½%

terms of loan (in years)

Amount	15	20	25	30	35	40
500	4,07	3,43	3,06	2,82	2,67	2,56
1 000	8,14	6,85	6,11	5,64	5,33	5,12
2 000	16,28	13,69	12,21	11,27	10,66	10,22
3 000	24,42	20,54	18,32	16,92	15,99	15,33
4 000	32,56	27,38	24,42	22,55	21,32	20,44
5 000	40,69	34,22	30,52	28,20	26,65	25,58
6 000	48,83	41,07	36,63	33,84	31,98	30,66
7 000	56,97	47,91	42,78	39,48	37,31	35,77
8 000	65,11	54,76	48,84	45,11	42,64	40,88
9 000	73,24	61,60	54,94	50,76	47,97	46,05
10 000	81,38	68,44	61,04	56,39	53,30	51,16
15 000	122,07	102,66	91,56	84,59	79,95	76,74
20 000	162,76	136,88	122,08	112,78	106,60	102,20
25 000	203,45	171,10	152,60	140,98	133,25	127,90
30 000	244,14	205,32	183,12	169,17	159,90	153,30
35 000	284,83	239,54	213,64	197,37	186,55	178,85
40 000	325,52	273,76	244,16	225,56	213,20	204,40
45 000	366,21	307,98	274,68	253,76	239,85	230,22
50 000	406,90	342,20	305,20	281,95	266,50	255,80
60 000	488,28	410,64	366,24	338,40	319,80	306,60
70 000	569,66	479,08	427,28	394,73	373,10	357,70
80 000	651,04	547,82	488,32	451,12	426,40	408,80
90 000	732,42	615,96	549,36	507,51	479,70	460,44
100 000	813,80	684,40	610,40	563,90	533,00	511,60

6% Required monthly payment to refund a mortgage loan

terms of loan (in years)

Amount	1	2	3	4	5	10
500	43,02	22,15	15,20	11,73	9,65	5,54
1 000	86,04	44,29	30,39	23,46	19,30	11,07
2 000	172,07	88,58	60,78	46,91	38,60	22,14
3 000	258,10	132,87	91,17	70,36	57,90	33,20
4 000	344,14	177,15	121,56	93,81	77,20	44,27
5 000	430,17	221,44	151,95	117,26	96,50	55,33
6 000	516,20	265,73	182,34	140,71	115,80	66,40
7 000	602,23	310,02	212,73	164,16	135,10	77,46
8 000	688,27	354,30	243,11	187,62	154,39	88,53
9 000	774,30	398,59	273,50	211,07	173,69	99,59
10 000	860,33	442,88	303,89	234,52	192,99	110,66
15 000	1290,49	664,32	455,83	351,77	289,48	165,98
20 000	1720,66	885,75	607,78	469,03	385,98	221,31
25 000	2150,82	1107,19	759,72	586,29	482,47	276,63
30 000	2580,98	1328,63	911,66	703,54	578,96	331,96
35 000	3011,15	1550,07	1063,61	820,80	675,46	387,28
40 000	3441,31	1771,50	1215,55	938,06	771,95	442,61
45 000	3871,47	1992,94	1367,49	1055,31	868,44	497,93
50 000	4301,63	2214,38	1519,43	1172,57	964,93	553,26
60 000	5161,96	2657,25	1823,32	1407,08	1157,92	663,91
70 000	6022,29	3100,13	2127,21	1641,59	1350,91	774,56
80 000	6882,61	3543,00	2431,09	1876,11	1543,89	885,21
90 000	7742,94	3985,87	2734,98	2110,62	1736,88	995,86
100 000	8603,26	4428,75	3038,86	2345,13	1929,86	1106,51

Required monthly payment to refund a mortgage loan

6%

terms of loan (in years)

Amount	15	20	25	30	35	40
500	4,20	3,57	3,20	2,98	2,83	2,73
1 000	8,40	7,13	6,40	5,95	5,66	5,46
2 000	16,80	14,25	12,80	11,90	11,31	10,91
3 000	25,20	21,37	19,20	17,85	16,96	16,36
4 000	33,60	28,49	25,60	23,80	22,62	21,81
5 000	42,00	35,61	32,00	29,75	28,27	27,26
6 000	50,40	42,74	38,39	35,69	33,92	32,71
7 000	58,80	49,86	44,79	41,64	39,57	38,16
8 000	67,20	56,98	51,19	47,59	45,23	43,61
9 000	75,59	64,10	57,59	53,54	50,88	49,06
10 000	83,99	71,22	63,99	59,49	56,53	54,51
15 000	125,99	106,83	95,98	89,23	84,79	81,77
20 000	167,98	142,44	127,97	118,97	113,06	109,02
25 000	209,98	178,05	159,96	148,71	141,32	136,28
30 000	251,97	213,66	191,95	178,45	169,58	163,53
35 000	293,96	249,27	223,94	208,19	197,84	190,79
40 000	335,96	284,88	255,93	237,93	226,11	218,04
45 000	377,95	320,49	287,92	267,68	254,37	245,29
50 000	419,95	356,10	319,91	297,42	282,63	272,55
60 000	503,93	427,32	383,89	356,90	339,16	327,06
70 000	587,92	498,54	447,87	416,38	395,68	381,57
80 000	671,91	569,76	511,85	475,86	452,21	436,08
90 000	755,90	640,97	575,83	535,35	508,73	490,58
100 000	839,89	712,19	639,81	594,83	565,26	545,09

6¼% Required monthly payment to refund a mortgage loan

terms of loan (in years)

Amount	1	2	3	4	5	10
500	43,07	22,20	15,25	11,78	9,71	5,59
1 000	86,14	44,40	30,50	23,56	19,41	11,19
2 000	172,29	88,79	61,00	47,13	38,82	22,38
3 000	258,43	133,19	91,50	70,69	58,24	33,56
4 000	344,58	177,59	122,00	94,25	77,65	44,75
5 000	430,72	221,99	152,50	117,82	97,06	55,94
6 000	516,87	266,38	182,99	141,38	116,47	67,13
7 000	603,01	310,78	213,49	164,94	135,88	78,31
8 000	689,16	355,18	243,99	188,50	155,30	89,50
9 000	775,30	399,58	274,49	212,07	174,71	100,69
10 000	861,45	443,97	304,99	235,63	194,12	111,88
15 000	1292,17	665,96	457,49	353,45	291,18	167,82
20 000	1722,89	887,95	609,98	471,26	388,24	223,75
25 000	2153,62	1109,93	762,48	589,08	485,30	279,69
30 000	2584,34	1331,92	914,97	706,89	582,36	335,63
35 000	3015,06	1553,91	1067,47	824,71	679,42	391,57
40 000	3445,79	1775,89	1219,96	942,52	776,48	447,51
45 000	3876,51	1997,88	1372,46	1060,34	873,54	503,45
50 000	4307,23	2219,87	1524,95	1178,16	970,60	559,38
60 000	5168,68	2663,84	1829,95	1413,79	1164,72	671,26
70 000	6030,13	3107,81	2134,94	1649,42	1358,84	783,14
80 000	6891,57	3551,79	2439,93	1885,05	1552,96	895,01
90 000	7753,02	3995,76	2744,92	2120,68	1747,08	1006,89
100 000	8614,47	4439,73	3049,91	2356,31	1941,20	1118,77

Required monthly payment to refund a mortgage loan $6^{1}/_{4}\%$

terms of loan (in years)

Amount	15	20	25	30	35	40
500	4,27	3,63	3,27	3,05	2,91	2,81
1 000	8,53	7,26	6,55	6,11	5,82	5,62
2 000	17,06	14,53	13,09	12,21	11,63	11,24
3 000	25,59	21,79	19,64	18,32	17,45	16,86
4 000	34,12	29,05	26,19	24,42	23,27	22,48
5 000	42,65	36,31	32,74	30,53	29,08	28,11
6 000	51,18	43,58	39,28	36,63	34,90	33,73
7 000	59,72	50,84	45,83	42,74	40,72	39,35
8 000	68,25	58,10	52,38	48,84	46,53	44,97
9 000	76,78	65,37	58,93	54,95	52,35	50,59
10 000	85,31	72,63	65,47	61,05	58,17	56,21
15 000	127,96	108,94	98,21	91,58	87,25	84,32
20 000	170,62	145,26	130,95	122,11	116,33	112,42
25 000	213,27	181,57	163,69	152,63	145,42	140,53
30 000	255,92	217,88	196,42	183,16	174,50	168,64
35 000	298,58	254,20	229,16	213,69	203,58	196,74
40 000	341,23	290,51	261,90	244,21	232,66	224,85
45 000	383,88	326,83	294,63	274,74	261,75	252,95
50 000	426,54	363,14	327,37	305,27	290,83	281,06
60 000	511,85	435,77	392,84	366,32	349,00	337,27
70 000	597,15	508,40	458,32	427,37	407,16	393,48
80 000	682,46	581,02	523,79	488,43	465,33	449,70
90 000	767,77	653,65	589,27	549,48	523,49	505,91
100 000	853,08	726,28	654,74	610,53	581,66	562,12

15

6½% Required monthly payment to refund a mortgage loan

terms of loan (in years)

Amount	1	2	3	4	5	10
500	43,13	22,26	15,31	11,84	9,77	5,66
1 000	86,26	44,51	30,61	23,68	19,53	11,32
2 000	172,52	89,02	61,22	47,36	39,06	22,63
3 000	258,78	133,53	91,83	71,03	58,58	33,94
4 000	345,03	178,03	122,44	94,71	78,11	45,25
5 000	431,29	222,54	153,05	118,38	97,63	56,56
6 000	517,55	267,05	183,66	142,06	117,16	67,87
7 000	603,80	311,56	214,27	165,73	136,69	79,18
8 000	690,06	356,06	244,88	189,41	156,21	90,49
9 000	776,32	400,57	275,49	213,08	175,74	101,80
10 000	862,57	445,08	306,10	236,76	195,26	113,11
15 000	1293,86	667,61	459,15	355,13	292,89	169,67
20 000	1725,14	890,15	612,20	473,51	390,52	226,22
25 000	2156,42	1112,69	765,25	591,88	488,15	282,78
30 000	2587,71	1335,22	918,30	710,26	585,78	339,33
35 000	3018,99	1557,76	1071,35	828,64	683,41	395,89
40 000	3450,27	1780,30	1224,39	947,01	781,03	452,44
45 000	3881,56	2002,83	1377,44	1065,39	878,66	509,00
50 000	4312,84	2225,37	1530,49	1183,76	976,29	565,55
60 000	5175,41	2670,44	1836,59	1420,51	1171,55	678,66
70 000	6037,97	3115,51	2142,69	1657,27	1366,81	791,97
80 000	6900,54	3560,59	2448,78	1894,02	1562,06	904,88
90 000	7763,11	4005,66	2754,88	2130,77	1757,32	1017,99
100 000	8625,67	4450,73	3060,98	2367,52	1952,58	1131,10

Required monthly payment to refund a mortgage loan 6½%

terms of loan (in years)

Amount	15	20	25	30	35	40
500	4,34	3,71	3,35	3,14	3,00	2,90
1 000	8,67	7,41	6,70	6,27	5,99	5,80
2 000	17,33	14,82	13,40	12,53	11,97	11,59
3 000	26,00	22,22	20,10	18,80	17,95	17,38
4 000	34,66	29,63	26,80	25,06	23,93	23,18
5 000	43,32	37,03	33,50	31,33	29,92	28,97
6 000	51,99	44,44	40,19	37,59	35,90	34,76
7 000	60,65	51,84	46,89	43,85	41,88	40,56
8 000	69,31	59,25	53,59	50,12	47,86	46,35
9 000	77,98	66,65	60,29	56,38	53,85	52,14
10 000	86,64	74,06	66,99	62,65	59,83	57,94
15 000	129,96	111,08	100,48	93,97	89,74	86,90
20 000	173,28	148,11	133,97	125,29	119,65	115,87
25 000	216,60	185,13	167,46	156,61	149,56	144,83
30 000	259,92	222,16	200,95	187,93	179,48	173,80
35 000	303,23	259,18	234,44	219,25	209,39	202,77
40 000	346,55	296,21	267,93	250,57	239,30	231,73
45 000	389,87	333,23	301,43	281,89	269,21	260,70
50 000	433,19	370,26	334,92	313,21	299,12	289,66
60 000	519,83	444,31	401,90	375,85	358,95	347,40
70 000	606,46	518,36	468,88	438,49	418,77	405,53
80 000	693,10	592,41	535,86	501,13	478,59	463,46
90 000	779,74	666,46	602,85	563,77	538,42	521,39
100 000	866,37	740,51	669,83	626,41	598,24	579,32

Required monthly payment to refund a mortgage loan

Amount	terms of loan (in years)					
	1	2	3	4	5	10
500	43,18	22,31	15,36	11,89	9,82	5,72
1 000	86,37	44,62	30,72	23,79	19,64	11,43
2 000	172,74	89,23	61,44	47,57	39,28	22,87
3 000	259,11	133,85	92,16	71,36	58,92	34,30
4 000	345,47	178,47	122,88	95,15	78,56	45,74
5 000	431,84	223,09	153,60	118,94	98,20	57,17
6 000	518,21	267,70	184,32	142,72	117,84	68,61
7 000	604,58	312,32	215,04	166,51	137,48	80,04
8 000	690,95	356,94	245,76	190,30	157,12	91,48
9 000	777,32	401,56	276,48	214,09	176,76	102,91
10 000	863,69	446,17	307,21	237,87	196,40	114,35
15 000	1295,53	669,26	460,81	356,81	294,60	171,52
20 000	1727,37	892,34	614,41	475,75	392,80	228,70
25 000	2159,22	1115,43	768,01	594,69	490,99	285,87
30 000	2591,06	1338,52	921,62	713,62	589,19	343,05
35 000	3022,90	1561,60	1075,22	832,56	687,39	400,22
40 000	3454,75	1784,69	1228,82	951,50	785,59	457,39
45 000	3886,59	2007,78	1382,42	1070,43	883,79	514,57
50 000	4318,43	2230,86	1536,03	1189,37	981,99	571,74
60 000	5182,12	2677,03	1843,23	1427,25	1178,39	686,09
70 000	6045,81	3123,21	2150,44	1665,12	1374,78	800,44
80 000	6909,50	3569,38	2457,64	1902,99	1571,18	914,79
90 000	7773,18	4015,55	2764,85	2140,87	1767,58	1029,14
100 000	8636,87	4461,72	3072,05	2378,74	1963,98	1143,48

Required monthly payment to refund a mortgage loan 6¾%

terms of loan (in years)

Amount	15	20	25	30	35	40
500	4,40	3,77	3,43	3,21	3,07	2,98
1 000	8,80	7,55	6,85	6,42	6,15	5,97
2 000	17,60	15,10	13,70	12,85	12,30	11,93
3 000	26,39	22,65	20,55	19,27	18,45	17,90
4 000	35,19	30,19	27,40	25,70	24,60	23,87
5 000	43,99	37,74	34,25	32,12	30,75	29,83
6 000	52,79	45,29	41,10	38,55	36,90	35,80
7 000	61,58	52,84	47,95	44,97	43,05	41,77
8 000	70,38	60,39	54,80	51,39	49,20	47,73
9 000	79,18	67,94	61,65	57,82	55,35	53,70
10 000	87,98	75,48	68,50	64,24	61,50	59,67
15 000	131,96	113,23	102,76	96,36	92,25	89,50
20 000	175,95	150,97	137,01	128,49	122,99	119,34
25 000	219,94	188,71	171,26	160,61	153,74	149,17
30 000	263,93	226,45	205,51	192,73	184,49	179,00
35 000	307,92	264,20	239,77	224,85	215,24	208,84
40 000	351,90	301,94	274,02	256,97	245,99	238,67
45 000	395,89	339,68	308,27	289,09	276,74	268,50
50 000	439,88	377,42	342,52	321,21	307,49	298,34
60 000	527,86	452,91	411,03	385,46	368,98	358,01
70 000	615,83	528,39	479,53	449,70	430,48	417,67
80 000	703,81	603,88	548,04	513,94	491,98	477,34
90 000	791,78	679,36	616,54	578,18	553,48	537,01
100 000	879,76	754,84	685,05	642,43	614,97	596,68

Required monthly payment to refund a mortgage loan

	terms of loan (in years)					
Amount	1	2	3	4	5	10
500	43,25	22,37	15,42	11,95	9,88	5,78
1 000	86,49	44,73	30,84	23,90	19,76	11,56
2 000	172,97	89,46	61,67	47,80	39,51	23,12
3 000	259,45	134,19	92,50	71,70	59,27	34,68
4 000	345,93	178,91	123,33	95,60	79,02	46,24
5 000	432,41	223,64	154,16	119,50	98,78	57,80
6 000	518,89	268,37	184,99	143,40	118,53	69,36
7 000	605,37	313,10	215,82	167,30	138,28	80,92
8 000	691,85	357,82	246,66	191,20	158,04	92,48
9 000	778,33	402,55	277,49	215,10	177,79	104,04
10 000	864,81	447,28	308,32	239,00	197,55	115,60
15 000	1297,22	670,91	462,48	358,50	296,32	173,40
20 000	1729,62	894,55	616,63	478,00	395,09	231,19
25 000	2162,02	1118,19	770,79	597,50	493,86	288,99
30 000	2594,43	1341,82	924,95	717,00	592,63	346,79
35 000	3026,83	1565,46	1079,10	836,50	691,40	404,58
40 000	3459,23	1789,10	1233,26	956,00	790,17	462,38
45 000	3891,64	2012,73	1387,42	1075,50	888,94	520,18
50 000	4324,04	2236,37	1541,58	1195,00	987,71	577,97
60 000	5188,85	2683,64	1849,89	1434,00	1185,25	693,57
70 000	6053,65	3130,91	2158,20	1673,00	1382,79	809,16
80 000	6918,46	3578,19	2466,52	1912,00	1580,33	924,76
90 000	7783,27	4025,46	2774,83	2151,00	1777,87	1040,35
100 000	8648,07	4472,73	3083,15	2389,99	1975,41	1155,94

Required monthly payment to refund a mortgage loan 7%

Amount	terms of loan (in years)					
	15	20	25	30	35	40
500	4,47	3,85	3,51	3,30	3,16	3,08
1 000	8,94	7,70	7,01	6,59	6,32	6,15
2 000	17,87	15,39	14,01	13,18	12,64	12,29
3 000	26,80	23,08	21,02	19,76	18,96	18,43
4 000	35,73	30,78	28,02	26,35	25,28	24,57
5 000	44,67	38,47	35,03	32,94	31,60	30,71
6 000	53,60	46,16	42,03	39,52	37,92	36,86
7 000	62,53	53,86	49,03	46,11	44,24	43,00
8 000	71,46	61,55	56,04	52,69	50,55	49,14
9 000	80,40	69,24	63,04	59,28	56,87	55,28
10 000	89,33	76,94	70,05	65,87	63,19	61,42
15 000	133,99	115,40	105,07	98,80	94,78	92,13
20 000	178,65	153,87	140,09	131,73	126,38	122,84
25 000	223,32	192,33	175,11	164,66	157,97	153,55
30 000	267,98	230,80	210,13	197,59	189,56	184,26
35 000	312,64	269,26	245,15	230,52	221,16	214,97
40 000	357,30	307,73	280,17	263,45	252,75	245,68
45 000	401,97	346,19	315,19	296,38	284,34	276,39
50 000	446,63	384,66	350,21	329,31	315,94	307,10
60 000	535,95	461,59	420,25	395,17	379,12	368,52
70 000	625,28	538,52	490,30	461,03	442,31	429,93
80 000	714,60	615,45	560,34	526,89	505,50	491,35
90 000	803,93	692,38	630,38	592,75	568,68	552,77
100 000	893,25	769,32	700,42	658,61	631,87	614,19

Required monthly payment to refund a mortgage loan

terms of loan (in years)

Amount	1	2	3	4	5	10
500	43,30	22,42	15,47	12,01	9,93	5,84
1 000	86,59	44,84	30,94	24,01	19,87	11,68
2 000	173,19	89,67	61,88	48,03	39,74	23,37
3 000	259,78	134,51	92,83	72,04	59,61	35,05
4 000	346,37	179,35	123,77	96,05	79,47	46,74
5 000	432,96	224,19	154,71	120,06	99,34	58,42
6 000	519,56	269,02	185,65	144,08	119,21	70,11
7 000	606,15	313,86	216,60	168,09	139,08	81,79
8 000	692,74	358,70	247,54	192,10	158,95	93,48
9 000	779,33	403,54	278,48	216,11	178,82	105,16
10 000	865,93	448,37	309,42	240,13	198,69	116,85
15 000	1298,89	672,56	464,14	360,19	298,03	175,27
20 000	1731,85	896,75	618,85	480,25	397,37	233,69
25 000	2164,82	1120,93	773,56	600,31	496,72	292,12
30 000	2597,78	1345,12	928,27	720,38	596,06	350,54
35 000	3030,74	1569,31	1082,99	840,44	695,40	408,96
40 000	3463,70	1793,49	1237,70	960,50	794,75	467,38
45 000	3896,67	2017,68	1392,41	1080,57	894,09	525,81
50 000	4329,63	2241,87	1547,12	1200,63	993,43	584,23
60 000	5195,56	2690,24	1856,55	1440,75	1192,12	701,08
70 000	6061,48	3138,62	2165,97	1680,88	1390,81	817,92
80 000	6927,41	3586,99	2475,40	1921,01	1589,49	934,77
90 000	7793,34	4035,36	2784,82	2161,13	1788,18	1051,61
100 000	8659,26	4483,74	3094,25	2401,26	1986,87	1168,46

Required monthly payment to refund a mortgage loan   7¼%

Amount	\multicolumn{6}{c}{terms of loan (in years)}					
	15	20	25	30	35	40
500	4,53	3,92	3,58	3,37	3,24	3,16
1 000	9,07	7,84	7,16	6,75	6,49	6,32
2 000	18,14	15,68	14,32	13,50	12,98	12,64
3 000	27,21	23,52	21,48	20,25	19,47	18,96
4 000	36,27	31,36	28,64	27,00	25,96	25,27
5 000	45,34	39,19	35,80	33,75	32,44	31,59
6 000	54,41	47,03	42,96	40,50	38,93	37,91
7 000	63,48	54,87	50,11	47,24	45,42	44,23
8 000	72,55	62,71	57,27	53,99	51,91	50,55
9 000	81,62	70,55	64,43	60,74	58,40	56,87
10 000	90,68	78,39	71,59	67,49	64,89	63,18
15 000	136,03	117,58	107,39	101,24	97,33	94,78
20 000	181,37	156,78	143,18	134,98	129,78	126,37
25 000	226,71	195,97	178,98	168,73	162,22	157,96
30 000	272,05	235,17	214,78	202,48	194,67	189,55
35 000	317,39	274,36	250,57	236,22	227,11	221,14
40 000	362,73	313,56	286,37	269,97	259,56	252,73
45 000	408,08	352,75	322,16	303,72	292,00	284,33
50 000	453,42	391,95	357,96	337,46	324,45	315,92
60 000	544,10	470,34	429,55	404,95	389,34	379,10
70 000	634,78	548,73	501,14	472,45	454,23	442,28
80 000	725,47	627,12	572,73	539,94	519,12	505,47
90 000	816,15	705,51	644,33	607,43	584,01	568,65
100 000	906,83	783,90	715,92	674,92	648,90	631,83

7½% Required monthly payment to refund a mortgage loan

Amount	terms of loan (in years)					
	1	2	3	4	5	10
500	43,36	22,48	15,53	12,07	10,00	5,91
1 000	86,71	44,95	31,06	24,13	19,99	11,82
2 000	173,41	89,90	62,11	48,26	39,97	23,63
3 000	260,12	134,85	93,17	72,38	59,96	35,44
4 000	346,82	179,80	124,22	96,51	79,94	47,25
5 000	433,53	224,74	155,27	120,63	99,92	59,06
6 000	520,23	269,69	186,33	144,76	119,91	70,87
7 000	606,94	314,64	217,38	168,88	139,89	82,68
8 000	693,64	359,59	248,43	193,01	159,87	94,49
9 000	780,35	404,53	279,49	217,13	179,86	106,30
10 000	867,05	449,48	310,54	241,26	199,94	118,11
15 000	1300,57	674,22	465,81	361,89	299,76	177,16
20 000	1734,10	898,96	621,08	482,51	399,68	236,21
25 000	2167,62	1123,69	776,35	603,14	499,59	295,27
30 000	2601,14	1348,43	931,61	723,77	599,51	354,32
35 000	3034,66	1573,17	1086,88	844,40	699,43	413,37
40 000	3468,19	1797,91	1242,15	965,02	799,35	472,42
45 000	3901,71	2022,64	1397,42	1085,65	899,26	531,48
50 000	4335,23	2247,38	1552,69	1206,28	999,18	590,53
60 000	5202,28	2696,86	1863,22	1447,53	1199,02	708,63
70 000	6069,32	3146,33	2173,76	1688,79	1398,85	826,74
80 000	6936,37	3595,81	2484,30	1930,04	1598,69	944,94
90 000	7803,41	4045,28	2794,83	2171,30	1798,52	1062,95
100 000	8670,46	4494,76	3105,37	2412,55	1998,36	1181,05

Required monthly payment to refund a mortgage loan

7½%

terms of loan (in years)

Amount	15	20	25	30	35	40
500	4,61	4,00	3,66	3,46	3,34	3,25
1 000	9,21	7,99	7,32	6,92	6,67	6,50
2 000	18,42	15,98	14,64	13,83	13,33	13,00
3 000	27,62	23,96	21,95	20,75	19,99	19,49
4 000	36,83	31,95	29,27	27,66	26,65	25,99
5 000	46,03	39,94	36,58	34,57	33,31	32,49
6 000	55,24	47,92	43,90	41,49	39,97	38,98
7 000	64,44	55,91	51,21	48,40	46,63	45,48
8 000	73,65	63,89	58,53	55,32	53,29	51,97
9 000	82,85	71,88	65,84	62,23	59,95	58,47
10 000	92,06	79,87	73,16	69,14	66,61	64,97
15 000	138,08	119,80	109,74	103,71	99,92	97,45
20 000	184,11	159,83	146,32	138,28	133,22	129,93
25 000	230,13	199,66	182,89	172,85	166,52	162,41
30 000	276,16	239,59	219,47	207,42	199,83	194,89
35 000	322,18	279,52	256,05	241,99	233,13	227,37
40 000	368,21	319,45	292,63	276,56	266,44	259,85
45 000	414,24	359,38	329,20	311,13	299,74	292,33
50 000	460,26	399,31	365,78	345,70	333,04	324,81
60 000	552,31	479,17	438,94	414,84	399,65	389,78
70 000	644,36	559,03	512,09	483,98	466,26	454,74
80 000	736,42	638,89	585,25	553,11	532,87	519,70
90 000	828,47	718,75	658,40	622,25	599,47	584,66
100 000	920,52	798,61	731,56	691,39	666,08	649,62

7¾% Required monthly payment to refund a mortgage loan

terms of loan (in years)

Amount	1	2	3	4	5	10
500	43,41	22,53	15,58	12,12	10,05	5,97
1 000	86,82	45,06	31,16	24,24	20,10	11,94
2 000	173,63	90,12	62,33	48,48	40,20	23,87
3 000	260,45	135,17	93,49	72,72	60,30	35,81
4 000	347,27	180,23	124,66	96,95	80,39	47,75
5 000	434,08	225,29	155,82	121,19	100,49	59,68
6 000	520,90	270,35	186,99	145,43	120,59	71,62
7 000	607,71	315,40	218,15	169,67	140,69	83,56
8 000	694,53	360,46	249,32	193,91	160,79	95,50
9 000	781,35	405,52	280,48	218,15	180,89	107,43
10 000	868,16	450,58	311,65	242,39	200,99	119,37
15 000	1302,25	675,87	467,47	363,58	30¡,48	179,05
20 000	1736,33	901,15	623,30	484,77	401,97	238,74
25 000	2170,41	1126,44	779,12	605,96	502,47	298,42
30 000	2604,49	1351,73	934,95	727,16	602,96	358,11
35 000	3038,57	1577,02	1090,77	848,35	703,45	417,79
40 000	3472,66	1802,31	1246,60	969,54	803,95	477,48
45 000	3906,74	2027,60	1402,42	1090,74	904,44	537,16
50 000	4340,82	2252,89	1558,25	1211,93	1004,94	596,85
60 000	5208,98	2703,46	1869,90	1454,31	1205,92	716,22
70 000	6077,15	3154,04	2181,54	1696,70	1406,91	835,59
80 000	6945,31	3604,62	2493,19	1939,09	1607,90	954,96
90 000	7813,48	4055,19	2804,84	2181,47	1808,88	1074,33
100 000	8681,64	4505,77	3116,49	2423,86	2009,87	1193,70

Required monthly payment to refund a mortgage loan   7¾%

Amount	terms of loan (in years)					
	15	20	25	30	35	40
500	4,67	4,07	3,74	3,54	3,42	3,34
1 000	9,34	8,13	7,47	7,08	6,83	6,68
2 000	18,69	16,27	14,95	14,16	13,67	13,35
3 000	28,03	24,40	22,42	21,24	20,50	20,03
4 000	37,37	32,54	29,89	28,32	27,34	26,70
5 000	46,71	40,67	37,37	35,40	34,17	33,38
6 000	56,06	48,81	44,84	42,48	41,00	40,05
7 000	65,40	56,94	52,31	49,56	47,84	46,73
8 000	74,74	65,07	59,79	56,64	54,67	53,40
9 000	84,09	73,21	67,26	63,72	61,50	60,08
10 000	93,43	81,34	74,73	70,80	68,34	66,75
15 000	140,14	122,01	112,10	106,20	102,51	100,13
20 000	186,86	162,68	149,46	141,60	136,68	133,51
25 000	233,57	203,36	186,83	177,00	170,85	166,88
30 000	280,29	244,03	224,20	212,39	205,02	200,26
35 000	327,00	284,70	261,56	247,79	239,19	233,64
40 000	373,71	325,37	298,93	283,19	273,35	267,01
45 000	420,43	366,04	336,29	318,59	307,52	300,39
50 000	467,14	406,71	373,66	353,99	341,69	333,77
60 000	560,57	488,05	448,39	424,79	410,03	400,52
70 000	654,00	569,40	523,12	495,59	478,37	467,27
80 000	747,43	650,74	597,86	566,39	546,71	534,03
90 000	840,86	732,08	672,59	637,18	615,05	600,78
100 000	934,29	813,42	747,32	707,98	683,39	667,53

27

8%

Required monthly payment to refund a mortgage loan

	terms of loan (in years)					
Amount	1	2	3	4	5	10
500	43,47	22,59	15,64	12,18	10,11	6,04
1 000	86,93	45,17	31,28	24,36	20,22	12,07
2 000	173,86	90,34	62,56	48,71	40,43	24,13
3 000	260,79	135,51	93,83	73,06	60,65	36,20
4 000	347,72	180,68	125,11	97,41	80,86	48,26
5 000	434,65	225,84	156,39	121,76	101,08	60,33
6 000	521,57	271,01	187,66	146,12	121,29	72,39
7 000	608,50	316,18	218,94	170,47	141,50	84,45
8 000	695,43	361,35	250,22	194,82	161,72	96,52
9 000	782,36	406,52	281,49	219,17	181,93	108,58
10 000	869,29	451,68	312,77	243,52	202,15	120,65
15 000	1303,93	677,52	469,15	365,28	303,22	180,97
20 000	1738,57	903,36	625,53	487,04	404,29	241,29
25 000	2173,21	1129,20	781,91	608,80	505,36	301,61
30 000	2607,85	1355,04	938,30	730,56	606,43	361,93
35 000	3042,49	1580,88	1094,68	852,32	707,50	422,25
40 000	3477,14	1806,72	1251,06	974,08	808,57	482,57
45 000	3911,78	2032,56	1407,44	1095,84	909,64	542,89
50 000	4346,42	2258,40	1563,82	1217,60	1010,71	603,21
60 000	5215,70	2710,08	1876,59	1461,12	1212,85	723,85
70 000	6084,98	3161,76	2189,35	1704,64	1415,00	844,49
80 000	6954,27	3613,44	2502,11	1948,15	1617,14	965,13
90 000	7823,55	4065,12	2814,88	2191,67	1819,28	1085,77
100 000	8692,83	4516,80	3127,64	2435,19	2021,42	1206,41

Required monthly payment to refund a mortgage loan
8%

Amount	15	20	25	30	35	40
500	4,75	4,15	3,82	3,63	3,51	3,43
1 000	9,49	8,29	7,64	7,25	7,01	6,86
2 000	18,97	16,57	15,27	14,50	14,02	13,72
3 000	28,45	24,86	22,90	21,75	21,03	20,57
4 000	37,93	33,14	30,53	28,99	28,04	27,43
5 000	47,41	41,42	38,17	36,24	35,05	34,28
6 000	56,89	49,71	45,80	43,49	42,05	41,14
7 000	66,38	57,99	53,43	50,73	49,06	47,99
8 000	75,86	66,27	61,06	57,98	56,07	54,85
9 000	85,34	74,56	68,69	65,23	63,08	61,71
10 000	94,82	82,84	76,33	72,48	70,09	68,56
15 000	142,23	124,26	114,49	108,71	105,13	102,84
20 000	189,64	165,68	152,65	144,95	140,17	137,12
25 000	237,04	207,09	190,81	181,18	175,21	171,40
30 000	284,45	248,51	228,97	217,42	210,25	205,67
35 000	331,86	289,93	267,13	253,65	245,29	239,95
40 000	379,27	331,35	305,29	289,89	280,34	274,23
45 000	426,67	372,77	343,45	326,12	315,38	308,51
50 000	474,08	414,18	381,61	362,36	350,42	342,79
60 000	568,90	497,02	457,93	434,83	420,50	411,34
70 000	663,71	579,86	534,25	507,30	490,58	479,90
80 000	758,53	662,69	610,58	579,77	560,67	548,45
90 000	853,34	745,53	686,90	652,24	630,75	617,01
100 000	948,16	828,36	763,22	724,72	700,83	685,57

Table header: terms of loan (in years)

8¼% Required monthly payment to refund a mortgage loan

terms of loan (in years)

Amount	1	2	3	4	5	10
500	43,52	22,64	15,69	12,23	10,16	6,10
1 000	87,04	45,28	31,39	24,47	20,33	12,19
2 000	174,08	90,56	62,78	48,93	40,66	24,38
3 000	261,12	135,83	94,16	73,40	60,99	36,58
4 000	348,16	181,11	125,55	97,86	81,32	48,77
5 000	435,20	226,39	156,94	122,33	101,65	60,96
6 000	522,24	271,67	188,33	146,79	121,98	73,15
7 000	609,28	316,95	219,72	171,26	142,31	85,34
8 000	696,32	362,23	251,10	195,72	162,64	97,53
9 000	783,36	407,50	282,49	220,19	182,97	109,73
10 000	870,40	452,78	313,88	244,65	203,30	121,92
15 000	1305,60	679,17	470,82	366,98	304,95	182,88
20 000	1740,80	905,56	627,76	489,31	406,60	243,84
25 000	2176,00	1131,96	784,70	611,63	508,25	304,80
30 000	2611,20	1358,35	941,64	733,96	609,90	365,76
35 000	3046,40	1584,74	1098,58	856,29	711,55	426,71
40 000	3481,60	1811,13	1255,52	978,62	813,20	487,67
45 000	3916,80	2037,52	1412,46	1100,94	914,84	548,63
50 000	4352,00	2263,91	1569,40	1223,27	1016,49	609,59
60 000	5222,40	2716,69	1883,27	1467,92	1219,79	731,51
70 000	6092,81	3169,48	2197,15	1712,58	1423,09	853,43
80 000	6963,21	3622,26	2511,03	1957,23	1626,39	975,35
90 000	7833,61	4075,04	2824,91	2201,88	1829,69	1097,27
100 000	8704,01	4527,82	3138,79	2446,54	2032,99	1219,18

Required monthly payment to refund a mortgage loan 8¼%

amount	terms of loan (in years)					
	15	20	25	30	35	40
500	4,81	4,22	3,90	3,71	3,59	3,52
1 000	9,62	8,43	7,79	7,42	7,18	7,04
2 000	19,24	16,87	15,58	14,83	14,37	14,07
3 000	28,86	25,30	23,38	22,25	21,55	21,11
4 000	38,48	33,74	31,17	29,66	28,74	28,15
5 000	48,11	42,17	38,96	37,08	35,92	35,19
6 000	57,73	50,60	46,75	44,49	43,10	42,22
7 000	67,35	59,04	54,55	51,91	50,29	49,26
8 000	76,97	67,47	62,34	59,33	57,47	56,30
9 000	86,59	75,91	70,13	66,74	64,65	63,33
10 000	96,21	84,34	77,92	74,16	71,84	70,37
15 000	144,32	126,51	116,88	111,23	107,76	105,56
20 000	192,42	168,68	155,85	148,31	143,68	140,74
25 000	240,53	210,85	194,81	185,39	179,60	175,93
30 000	288,63	253,02	233,77	222,47	215,52	211,11
35 000	336,74	295,19	272,73	259,55	251,44	246,30
40 000	384,84	337,36	311,69	296,63	287,35	281,48
45 000	432,95	379,53	350,65	333,70	323,27	316,67
50 000	481,06	421,70	389,61	370,78	359,19	351,85
60 000	577,27	506,04	467,54	444,94	431,03	422,22
70 000	673,48	590,38	545,46	519,10	502,87	492,59
80 000	769,69	674,72	623,38	593,25	574,71	562,96
90 000	865,90	759,06	701,31	667,41	646,55	633,34
100 000	962,11	843,40	779,23	741,56	718,39	703,71

8½% Required monthly payment to refund a mortgage loan

Amount	terms of loan (in years)					
	1	2	3	4	5	10
500	43,58	22,70	15,75	12,29	10,23	6,17
1 000	87,16	45,39	31,50	24,58	20,45	12,33
2 000	174,31	90,78	63,00	49,16	40,90	24,65
3 000	261,46	136,17	94,50	73,74	61,34	36,97
4 000	348,61	181,56	126,00	98,32	81,79	49,29
5 000	435,76	226,95	157,50	122,90	102,23	61,61
6 000	522,92	272,34	189,00	147,48	122,68	73,93
7 000	610,07	317,73	220,50	172,06	143,13	86,25
8 000	697,22	363,11	252,00	196,64	163,57	98,57
9 000	784,37	408,50	283,50	221,22	184,02	110,89
10 000	871,52	453,89	315,00	245,80	204,46	123,21
15 000	1307,28	680,83	472,50	368,69	306,69	184,81
20 000	1743,04	907,78	630,00	491,59	408,92	246,41
25 000	2178,80	1134,72	787,49	614,48	511,15	308,01
30 000	2614,56	1361,66	944,99	737,38	613,38	369,61
35 000	3050,32	1588,61	1102,49	860,27	715,61	431,21
40 000	3486,08	1815,55	1259,99	983,17	817,84	492,81
45 000	3921,84	2042,49	1417,49	1106,06	920,07	554,42
50 000	4357,60	2269,43	1574,98	1228,96	1022,30	616,02
60 000	5229,12	2723,32	1889,98	1474,75	1226,76	739,22
70 000	6100,63	3177,21	2204,98	1720,54	1431,22	862,42
80 000	6972,15	3631,09	2519,97	1966,33	1635,68	985,62
90 000	7843,67	4084,98	2834,97	2212,12	1840,13	1108,83
100 000	8715.19	4538.86	3149,96	2457,91	2044,59	1232,03

32

Required monthly payment to refund a mortgage loan

8½%

Amount	terms of loan (in years)					
	15	**20**	**25**	**30**	**35**	**40**
500	4,89	4,30	3,98	3,80	3,69	3,61
1 000	9,77	8,59	7,96	7,59	7,37	7,22
2 000	19,53	17,18	15,91	15,18	14,73	14,44
3 000	29,29	25,76	23,87	22,76	22,09	21,66
4 000	39,05	34,35	31,82	30,35	29,45	28,88
5 000	48,81	42,93	39,77	37,93	36,81	36,10
6 000	58,57	51,52	47,73	45,52	44,17	43,32
7 000	68,34	60,10	55,68	53,10	51,53	50,54
8 000	78,10	68,69	63,63	60,69	58,89	57,76
9 000	87,86	77,28	71,59	68,27	66,25	64,98
10 000	97,62	85,86	79,54	75,86	73,61	72,20
15 000	146,43	128,79	119,31	113,79	110,41	108,30
20 000	195,24	171,72	159,08	151,71	147,22	144,40
25 000	244,04	214,64	198,85	189,64	184,02	180,49
30 000	292,85	257,57	238,61	227,57	220,82	216,59
35 000	341,66	300,50	278,38	265,49	257,63	252,69
40 000	390,47	343,43	318,15	303,42	294,43	288,79
45 000	439,28	386,36	357,92	341,35	331,23	324,88
50 000	488,08	429,28	397,69	379,27	368,04	360,98
60 000	585,70	515,14	477,22	455,13	441,64	433,18
70 000	683,32	601,00	556,76	530,98	515,25	505,37
80 000	780,93	686,85	636,30	606,84	588,86	577,57
90 000	878,55	772,71	715,83	682,69	662,46	649,76
100 000	976,16	858,56	795,37	758,54	736,07	721,96

	terms of loan (in years)					
Amount	**1**	**2**	**3**	**4**	**5**	**10**
500	43,63	22,75	15,81	12,35	10,28	6,22
1 000	87,26	45,50	31,61	24,69	20,56	12,45
2 000	174,53	91,00	63,22	49,39	41,12	24,90
3 000	261,79	136,50	94,83	74,08	61,69	37,35
4 000	349,05	182,00	126,45	98,77	82,25	49,80
5 000	436,32	227,49	158,06	123,47	102,81	62,25
6 000	523,58	272,99	189,67	148,16	123,37	74,70
7 000	610,85	318,49	221,28	172,85	143,94	87,14
8 000	698,11	363,99	252,89	197,54	164,50	99,59
9 000	785,37	409,49	284,50	222,24	185,06	112,04
10 000	872,64	454,99	316,11	246,93	205,62	124,49
15 000	1308,95	682,48	474,17	370,40	308,43	186,74
20 000	1745,27	909,98	632,23	493,86	411,24	248,98
25 000	2181,59	1137,47	790,29	617,33	514,05	311,23
30 000	2617,91	1364,97	948,34	740,79	616,87	373,48
35 000	3054,23	1592,46	1106,40	864,26	719,68	435,72
40 000	3490,54	1819,96	1264,46	987,72	822,49	497,97
45 000	3926,86	2047,45	1422,51	1111,19	925,30	560,22
50 000	4363,18	2274,95	1580,57	1234,65	1028,11	622,46
60 000	5235,82	2729,94	1896,68	1481,58	1233,73	746,95
70 000	6108,45	3184,93	2212,80	1728,51	1439,35	871,45
80 000	6981,09	3639,92	2528,91	1975,44	1644,97	995,94
90 000	7853,72	4094,91	2845,03	2222,37	1850,60	1120,43
100 000	8726,36	4549,90	3161,14	2469,30	2056,22	1244,92

Required monthly payment to refund a mortgage loan 8¾%

	terms of loan (in years)					
Amount	15	20	25	30	35	40
500	4,95	4,37	4,06	3,88	3,77	3,70
1 000	9,90	8,74	8,12	7,76	7,54	7,40
2 000	19,81	17,48	16,23	15,51	15,08	14,81
3 000	29,71	26,21	24,35	23,27	22,62	22,21
4 000	39,61	34,95	32,46	31,03	30,15	29,61
5 000	49,51	43,69	40,58	38,78	37,69	37,02
6 000	59,42	52,43	48,70	46,54	45,23	44,42
7 000	69,32	61,17	56,81	54,29	52,77	51,82
8 000	79,22	69,91	64,93	62,05	60,31	59,22
9 000	89,13	78,64	73,05	69,81	67,85	66,63
10 000	99,03	87,38	81,16	77,56	75,38	74,03
15 000	148,54	131,07	121,74	116,34	113,08	111,05
20 000	198,06	174,76	162,32	155,13	150,77	148,06
25 000	247,57	218,46	202,90	193,91	188,46	185,08
30 000	297,09	262,15	243,48	232,69	226,15	222,09
35 000	346,60	305,84	284,06	271,47	263,85	259,11
40 000	396,12	349,53	324,65	310,25	301,54	296,12
45 000	445,63	393,22	365,23	349,03	339,23	333,14
50 000	495,15	436,91	405,81	387,82	376,92	370,15
60 000	594,18	524,29	486,97	465,38	452,31	444,18
70 000	693,21	611,68	568,13	542,94	527,69	518,21
80 000	792,24	699,06	649,29	620,50	603,08	592,24
90 000	891,27	786,44	730,45	698,07	678,46	666,27
100 000	990,29	873,82	811,61	775,63	753,85	740,30

Required monthly payment to refund a mortgage loan

terms of loan (in years)

Amount	1	2	3	4	5	10
500	43,69	22,81	15,87	12,41	10,34	6,29
1 000	87,38	45,61	31,73	24,81	20,68	12,58
2 000	174,76	91,22	63,45	49,62	41,36	25,16
3 000	262,13	136,83	95,18	74,43	62,04	37,74
4 000	349,51	182,44	126,90	99,23	82,72	50,32
5 000	436,88	228,05	158,62	124,04	103,40	62,90
6 000	524,26	273,66	190,35	148,85	124,08	75,48
7 000	611,63	319,27	222,07	173,65	144,76	88,06
8 000	699,01	364,88	253,79	198,46	165,43	100,64
9 000	786,38	410,49	285,52	223,27	186,11	113,21
10 000	873,76	456,10	317,24	248,08	206,79	125,79
15 000	1310,63	684,15	475,86	372,11	310,19	188,69
20 000	1747,51	912,19	634,47	496,15	413,58	251,58
25 000	2184,39	1140,24	793,09	620,18	516,97	314,48
30 000	2621,26	1368,29	951,71	744,22	620,37	377,37
35 000	3058,14	1596,33	1110,32	868,25	723,76	440,26
40 000	3495,02	1824,38	1268,94	992,29	827,15	503,16
45 000	3931,89	2052,43	1427,56	1116,33	930,55	566,05
50 000	4368,77	2280,48	1586,17	1240,36	1033,94	628,95
60 000	5242,52	2736,57	1903,41	1488,43	1240,73	754,74
70 000	6116,28	3192,66	2220,64	1736,50	1447,52	880,52
80 000	6990,03	3648,76	2537,87	1984,57	1654,30	1006,31
90 000	7863,78	4104,85	2855,11	2232,65	1861,09	1132,10
100 000	8737,54	4560,95	3172,34	2480,72	2067,88	1257,89

Required monthly payment to refund a mortgage loan

9%

terms of loan (in years)

Amount	15	20	25	30	35	40
500	5,03	4,45	4,14	3,97	3,86	3,80
1 000	10,05	8,90	8,28	7,93	7,72	7,59
2 000	20,10	17,79	16,56	15,86	15,44	15,18
3 000	30,14	26,68	24,84	23,79	23,16	22,77
4 000	40,19	35,57	33,12	31,72	30,87	30,35
5 000	50,23	44,46	41,40	39,65	38,59	37,94
6 000	60,28	53,36	49,68	47,57	46,31	45,53
7 000	70,32	62,25	57,96	55,50	54,03	53,12
8 000	80,37	71,14	66,24	63,43	61,74	60,70
9 000	90,41	80,03	74,52	71,36	69,46	68,29
10 000	100,46	88,92	82,80	79,29	77,18	75,88
15 000	150,68	133,38	124,20	118,93	115,77	113,82
20 000	200,91	177,84	165,60	158,57	154,35	151,75
25 000	251,13	222,30	207,00	198,21	192,94	189,69
30 000	301,36	266,76	248,40	237,85	231,53	227,63
35 000	351,59	311,22	289,80	277,50	270,11	265,56
40 000	401,81	355,68	331,20	317,14	308,70	303,50
45 000	452,04	400,14	372,59	356,78	347,29	341,44
50 000	502,26	444,60	413,99	396,42	385,87	379,38
60 000	602,72	533,52	496,79	475,70	463,05	455,25
70 000	703,17	622,44	579,59	554,99	540,22	531,12
80 000	803,62	711,36	662,39	634,27	617,40	607,00
90 000	904,07	800,28	745,18	713,55	694,57	682,87
100 000	1004,52	889,19	827,98	792,84	771,74	758,75

9¼% Required monthly payment to refund a mortgage loan

terms of loan (in years)

Amount	1	2	3	4	5	10
500	43,74	22,86	15,92	12,46	10,40	6,35
1 000	87,49	45,72	31,84	24,92	20,80	12,71
2 000	174,97	91,44	63,67	49,84	41,59	25,42
3 000	262,46	137,16	95,51	74,76	62,39	38,13
4 000	349,95	182,88	127,34	99,69	83,18	50,84
5 000	437,44	228,60	159,18	124,61	103,98	63,55
6 000	524,92	274,32	191,01	149,53	124,77	76,25
7 000	612,41	320,04	222,85	174,45	145,57	88,96
8 000	699,90	365,76	254,68	199,37	166,36	101,67
9 000	787,38	411,48	286,52	224,29	187,16	114,38
10 000	874,87	457,20	318,35	249,21	207,96	127,09
15 000	1312,31	685,80	477,53	373,82	311,93	190,64
20 000	1749,74	914,40	636,71	498,43	415,91	254,18
25 000	2187,18	1143,00	795,89	623,04	519,89	317,73
30 000	2624,61	1371,60	955,06	747,64	623,87	381,27
35 000	3062,05	1600,20	1114,24	872,25	727,84	444,82
40 000	3499,48	1828,80	1273,42	996,86	831,82	508,36
45 000	3936,92	2057,40	1432,59	1121,46	935,80	571,91
50 000	4374,35	2286,00	1591,77	1246,07	1039,78	635,45
60 000	5249,22	2743,19	1910,12	1495,29	1247,73	762,54
70 000	6124,09	3200,39	2228,48	1744,50	1455,69	889,64
80 000	6998,96	3657,59	2546,83	1993,72	1663,65	1016,73
90 000	7873,83	4114,79	2865,19	2242,93	1871,60	1143,82
100 000	8748,70	4571,99	3183,54	2492,14	2079,56	1270,91

Required monthly payment to refund a mortgage loan 9¼%

terms of loan (in years)

Amount	15	20	25	30	35	40
500	5,09	4,52	4,22	4,05	3,95	3,89
1 000	10,19	9,05	8,44	8,10	7,90	7,77
2 000	20,38	18,09	16,89	16,20	15,79	15,55
3 000	30,56	27,14	25,33	24,30	23,69	23,32
4 000	40,75	36,19	33,78	32,41	31,59	31,09
5 000	50,94	45,23	42,22	40,51	39,49	38,86
6 000	61,13	54,28	50,67	48,61	47,38	46,64
7 000	71,32	63,33	59,11	56,71	55,28	54,41
8 000	81,51	72,37	67,56	64,81	63,18	62,18
9 000	91,69	81,42	76,00	72,91	71,08	69,95
10 000	101,88	90,47	84,44	81,01	78,97	77,73
15 000	152,82	135,70	126,67	121,52	118,46	116,59
20 000	203,77	180,93	168,89	162,03	157,95	155,45
25 000	254,71	226,16	211,11	202,54	197,43	194,32
30 000	305,65	271,40	253,33	243,04	236,92	233,18
35 000	356,59	316,63	295,56	283,55	276,40	272,04
40 000	407,53	361,86	337,78	324,06	315,89	310,91
45 000	458,47	407,10	380,00	364,56	355,38	349,77
50 000	509,41	452,33	422,22	405,07	394,86	388,63
60 000	611,30	542,80	506,67	486,09	473,84	466,36
70 000	713,18	633,26	591,11	567,10	552,81	544,09
80 000	815,06	723,73	675,56	648,11	631,78	621,81
90 000	916,95	814,19	760,00	729,13	710,75	699,54
100 000	1018,83	904,66	844,45	810,14	789,73	777,27

9½% Required monthly payment to refund a mortgage loan

Amount	\multicolumn{6}{c}{terms of loan (in years)}
	1	2	3	4	5	10
500	43,80	22,92	15,98	12,52	10,46	6,42
1 000	87,60	45,84	31,95	25,04	20,92	12,84
2 000	175,20	91,67	63,90	50,08	41,83	25,68
3 000	262,80	137,50	95,85	75,11	62,74	38,52
4 000	350,40	183,33	127,80	100,15	83,66	51,36
5 000	438,00	229,16	159,74	125,18	104,57	64,20
6 000	525,60	274,99	191,69	150,22	125,48	77,04
7 000	613,20	320,82	223,64	175,26	146,39	89,88
8 000	700,79	366,65	255,59	200,29	167,31	102,72
9 000	788,39	412,48	287,53	225,33	188,22	115,56
10 000	875,99	458,31	319,48	250,36	209,13	128,40
15 000	1313,99	687,46	479,22	375,54	313,70	192,60
20 000	1751,98	916,61	638,96	500,72	418,26	256,80
25 000	2189,97	1145,77	798,69	625,90	522,82	321,00
30 000	2627,97	1374,92	958,43	751,08	627,39	385,20
35 000	3065,96	1604,07	1118,17	876,26	731,95	449,40
40 000	3503,95	1833,22	1277,91	1001,44	836,51	513,60
45 000	3941,95	2062,37	1437,65	1126,62	941,08	577,80
50 000	4379,94	2291,53	1597,38	1251,80	1045,64	642,00
60 000	5255,93	2749,83	1916,86	1502,16	1254,77	770,40
70 000	6131,91	3208,14	2236,34	1752,52	1463,89	898,80
80 000	7007,90	3666,44	2555,81	2002,88	1673,02	1027,20
90 000	7883,89	4124,74	2875,29	2253,24	1882,15	1155,60
100 000	8759,87	4583,05	3194,76	2503,60	2091,27	1284,00

Required monthly payment to refund a mortgage loan

9½%

terms of loan (in years)

Amount	15	20	25	30	35	40
500	5,17	4,61	4,31	4,14	4,04	3,98
1 000	10,34	9,21	8,62	8,28	8,08	7,96
2 000	20,67	18,41	17,23	16,56	16,16	15,92
3 000	31,00	27,61	25,84	24,83	24,24	23,88
4 000	41,33	36,81	34,45	33,11	32,32	31,84
5 000	51,67	46,02	43,06	41,38	40,40	39,80
6 000	62,00	55,22	51,67	49,66	48,47	47,76
7 000	72,33	64,42	60,28	57,93	56,55	55,72
8 000	82,66	*73,62	68,89	66,21	64,63	63,67
9 000	93,00	82,83	77,50	74,48	72,71	71,63
10 000	103,33	92,03	86,11	82,76	80,79	79,59
15 000	154,99	138,04	129,16	124,14	121,18	119,39
20 000	206,65	184,05	172,21	165,52	161,57	159,18
25 000	258,31	230,06	215,26	206,89	201,96	198,97
30 000	309,97	276,07	258,31	248,27	242,35	238,77
35 000	361,63	322,09	301,36	289,65	282,74	278,56
40 000	413,30	368,10	344,42	331,03	323,13	318,35
45 000	464,96	414,11	387,47	372,40	363,52	358,15
50 000	516,62	460,12	430,52	413,78	403,91	397,94
60 000	619,94	552,14	516,62	496,54	484,69	477,53
70 000	723,26	644,17	602,72	579,29	565,47	557,11
80 000	826,59	736,19	688,83	662,05	646,25	636,70
90 000	929,91	828,21	774,93	744,80	727,03	716,29
100 000	1033,23	920,24	861,03	827,56	807,81	795,88

9¾%

Required monthly payment to refund a mortgage loan

terms of loan (in years)

Amount	1	2	3	4	5	10
500	43,86	22,97	16,03	12,58	10,52	6,49
1 000	87,71	45,94	32,06	25,15	21,03	12,97
2 000	175,42	91,88	64,12	50,30	42,06	25,94
3 000	263,13	137,82	96,18	75,45	63,09	38,91
4 000	350,84	183,76	128,24	100,60	84,12	51,89
5 000	438,55	229,71	160,30	125,75	105,15	64,86
6 000	526,26	275,65	192,36	150,90	126,18	77,83
7 000	613,97	321,59	224,42	176,05	147,21	90,80
8 000	701,68	367,53	256,48	201,21	168,24	103,77
9 000	789,39	413,47	288,54	226,36	189,27	116,74
10 000	877,10	459,41	320,60	251,51	210,30	129,71
15 000	1315,65	689,12	480,90	377,26	315,45	194,57
20 000	1754,21	918,82	641,20	503,01	420,60	259,43
25 000	2192,76	1148,53	801,50	628,77	525,75	324,28
30 000	2631,31	1378,23	961,80	754,52	630,90	389,14
35 000	3069,86	1607,94	1122,10	880,27	736,05	454,00
40 000	3508,41	1837,64	1282,40	1006,03	841,20	518,85
45 000	3946,96	2067,35	1442,70	1131,78	946,35	583,71
50 000	4385,51	2297,05	1603,00	1257,53	1051,50	648,57
60 000	5262,62	2756,46	1923,59	1509,04	1261,80	778,28
70 000	6139,72	3215,87	2244,19	1760,55	1472,10	907,99
80 000	7016,82	3675,28	2564,79	2012,05	1682,40	1037,71
90 000	7893,93	4134,69	2885,39	2263,56	1892,70	1167,42
100 000	8771,03	4594,10	3205,99	2515,07	2103,00	1297,13

Required monthly payment to refund a mortgage loan $9\frac{3}{4}\%$

terms of loan (in years)

Amount	15	20	25	30	35	40
500	5,24	4,68	4,39	4,23	4,13	4,07
1 000	10,48	9,36	8,78	8,45	8,26	8,15
2 000	20,95	18,72	17,55	16,90	16,52	16,29
3 000	31,43	28,08	26,33	25,35	24,78	24,44
4 000	41,91	37,44	35,11	33,80	33,04	32,58
5 000	52,39	46,79	43,89	42,25	41,30	40,73
6 000	62,86	56,15	52,66	50,70	49,56	48,87
7 000	73,34	65,51	61,44	59,15	57,82	57,02
8 000	83,82	74,87	70,22	67,61	66,08	65,16
9 000	94,29	84,23	78,99	76,06	74,34	73,31
10 000	104,77	93,59	87,77	84,51	82,60	81,45
15 000	157,16	140,38	131,66	126,76	123,90	122,18
20 000	209,54	187,18	175,54	169,01	165,20	162,91
25 000	261,93	233,97	219,43	211,27	206,49	203,64
30 000	314,31	280,77	263,31	253,52	247,79	244,36
35 000	366,70	327,56	307,20	295,77	289,09	285,09
40 000	419,08	374,36	351,08	338,03	330,39	325,82
45 000	471,47	421,15	394,97	380,28	371,69	366,55
50 000	523,85	467,95	438,85	422,53	412,99	407,27
60 000	628,62	561,54	526,62	507,04	495,59	488,73
70 000	733,39	655,13	614,40	591,54	578,19	570,18
80 000	838,17	748,72	702,17	676,05	660,78	651,64
90 000	942,94	842,31	789,94	760,56	743,38	733,09
100 000	1047,71	935,90	877,71	845,06	825,98	814,55

10% Required monthly payment to refund a mortgage loan

Amount	terms of loan (in years)					
	1	2	3	4	5	10
500	43,92	23,03	16,09	12,64	10,58	6,56
1 000	87,83	46,06	32,18	25,27	21,15	13,11
2 000	175,65	92,11	64,35	50,54	42,30	26,21
3 000	263,47	138,16	96,52	75,80	63,45	39,32
4 000	351,29	184,21	128,69	101,07	84,60	52,42
5 000	439,11	230,26	160,87	126,33	105,74	65,52
6 000	526,94	276,31	193,04	151,60	126,89	78,63
7 000	614,76	322,37	225,21	176,86	148,04	91,73
8 000	702,58	368,42	257,38	202,13	169,19	104,83
9 000	790,40	414,47	289,56	227,40	190,33	117,94
10 000	878,22	460,52	321,73	252,66	211,48	131,04
15 000	1317,33	690,78	482,59	378,99	317,22	196,56
20 000	1756,44	921,04	643,45	505,32	422,96	262,07
25 000	2195,55	1151,30	804,31	631,64	528,70	327,59
30 000	2634,66	1381,55	965,18	757,90	634,44	393,11
35 000	3073,77	1611,81	1126,04	884,30	740,17	458,62
40 000	3512,88	1842,07	1286,90	1010,63	845,91	524,14
45 000	3951,99	2072,33	1447,76	1136,96	951,65	589,66
50 000	4391,10	2302,59	1608,62	1263,28	1057,39	655,17
60 000	5269,32	2763,10	1930,35	1515,94	1268,87	786,21
70 000	6147,54	3223,62	2252,07	1768,60	1480,34	917,24
80 000	7025,76	3684,14	2573,79	2021,25	1691,82	1048,27
90 000	7903,97	4144,65	2895,52	2273,91	1903,30	1179,31
100 000	8782,19	4605,17	3217,24	2526,56	2114,77	1310,34

Required monthly payment to refund a mortgage loan

10%

Amount	15	20	25	30	35	40
	terms of loan (in years)					
500	5,32	4,76	4,48	4,32	4,23	4,17
1 000	10,63	9,52	8,95	8,63	8,45	8,34
2 000	21,25	19,04	17,89	17,26	16,89	16,67
3 000	31,87	28,55	26,84	25,89	25,33	25,00
4 000	42,50	38,07	35,78	34,51	33,77	33,34
5 000	53,12	47,59	44,73	43,14	42,22	41,67
6 000	63,74	57,10	53,67	51,77	50,66	50,00
7 000	74,36	66,62	62,62	60,39	59,10	58,34
8 000	84,99	76,14	71,56	69,02	67,54	66,67
9 000	95,61	85,65	80,51	77,65	75,99	75,00
10 000	106,23	95,17	89,45	86,27	84,43	83,33
15 000	159,35	142,75	134,18	129,41	126,64	125,00
20 000	212,46	190,34	178,90	172,54	168,85	166,66
25 000	265,57	237,92	223,63	215,67	211,06	208,33
30 000	318,69	285,50	268,35	258,81	253,27	249,99
35 000	371,80	333,09	313,08	301,94	295,49	291,66
40 000	424,91	380,67	357,80	345,07	337,70	333,32
45 000	478,03	428,25	402,52	388,21	379,91	374,99
50 000	531,14	475,84	447,25	431,34	422,12	416,65
60 000	637,37	571,00	536,70	517,61	506,54	499,98
70 000	743,59	666,17	626,15	603,87	590,97	583,31
80 000	849,82	761,34	715,59	690,14	675,39	666,64
90 000	956,05	856,50	805,04	776,41	759,81	749,97
100 000	1062,27	951,67	894,49	862,67	844,24	833,30

10¼% Required monthly payment to refund a mortgage loan

terms of loan (in years)

Amount	1	2	3	4	5	10
500	43,97	23,09	16,15	12,70	10,64	6,62
1 000	87,94	46,17	32,29	25,39	21,27	13,24
2 000	175,87	92,33	64,57	50,77	42,54	26,48
3 000	263,81	138,49	96,86	76,15	63,80	39,71
4 000	351,74	184,65	129,14	101,53	85,07	52,95
5 000	439,67	230,82	161,43	126,91	106,33	66,18
6 000	527,61	276,98	193,71	152,29	127,60	79,42
7 000	615,54	323,14	226,00	177,67	148,86	92,66
8 000	703,47	369,30	258,28	203,05	170,13	105,89
9 000	791,41	415,47	290,57	228,43	191,40	119,13
10 000	879,34	461,63	322,85	253,81	212,66	132,36
15 000	1319,01	692,44	484,28	380,72	318,99	198,54
20 000	1758,67	923,25	645,70	507,62	425,32	264,72
25 000	2198,34	1154,06	807,13	634,52	531,65	330,90
30 000	2638,01	1384,88	968,55	761,43	637,97	397,08
35 000	3077,68	1615,69	1129,98	888,33	744,30	463,26
40 000	3517,34	1846,50	1291,40	1015,23	850,63	529,44
45 000	3957,01	2077,31	1452,83	1142,14	956,96	595,62
50 000	4396,68	2308,12	1614,25	1269,04	1063,29	661,80
60 000	5276,01	2769,75	1937,10	1522,85	1275,94	794,16
70 000	6155,35	3231,37	2259,95	1776,65	1488,60	926,52
80 000	7034,68	3692,99	2582,80	2030,46	1701,25	1058,88
90 000	7914,01	4154,62	2905,65	2284,27	1913,91	1191,24
100 000	8793,35	4616,24	3228,50	2538,08	2126,57	1323,60

Required monthly payment to refund a mortgage loan   10¼%

Amount	terms of loan (in years)					
	15	20	25	30	35	40
500	5,39	4,84	4,56	4,41	4,32	4,27
1 000	10,77	9,68	9,12	8,81	8,63	8,53
2 000	21,54	19,36	18,23	17,61	17,26	17,05
3 000	32,31	29,03	27,35	26,42	25,88	25,57
4 000	43,08	38,71	36,46	35,22	34,51	34,09
5 000	53,85	48,38	45,57	44,02	43,13	42,61
6 000	64,62	58,06	54,69	52,83	51,76	51,13
7 000	75,39	67,73	63,80	61,63	60,38	59,65
8 000	86,16	77,41	72,91	70,43	69,01	68,17
9 000	96,93	87,08	82,03	79,24	77,64	76,69
10 000	107,70	96,76	91,14	88,04	86,26	85,22
15 000	161,54	145,13	136,71	132,06	129,39	127,82
20 000	215,39	193,51	182,28	176,08	172,52	170,43
25 000	269,23	241,89	227,85	220,10	215,65	213,03
30 000	323,08	290,26	273,41	264,11	258,77	255,64
35 000	376,93	338,64	318,98	308,13	301,90	298,24
40 000	430,77	387,01	364,55	352,15	345,03	340,85
45 000	484,62	435,39	410,12	396,17	388,16	383,45
50 000	538,46	483,77	455,69	440,19	431,29	426,06
60 000	646,15	580,52	546,82	528,22	517,54	511,27
70 000	753,85	677,27	637,96	616,26	603,80	596,48
80 000	861,54	774,02	729,09	704,29	690,05	681,69
90 000	969,23	870,78	820,23	792,33	776,31	766,90
100 000	1076,92	967,53	911,37	880,37	862,57	852,11

10½% Required monthly payment to refund a mortgage loan

terms of loan (in years)

Amount	1	2	3	4	5	10
500	44,03	23,14	16,20	12,75	10,70	6,69
1 000	88,05	46,28	32,40	25,50	21,39	13,37
2 000	176,09	92,55	64,80	51,00	42,77	26,74
3 000	264,14	138,82	97,20	76,49	64,16	40,11
4 000	352,18	185,10	129,60	101,99	85,54	53,48
5 000	440,23	231,37	161,99	127,49	106,92	66,85
6 000	528,27	277,64	194,39	152,98	128,31	80,22
7 000	616,32	323,92	226,79	168,48	149,69	93,59
8 000	704,36	370,19	259,19	203,97	171,08	106,96
9 000	792,41	416,46	291,58	229,47	192,46	120,33
10 000	880,45	462,74	323,98	254,97	213,84	133,70
15 000	1320,68	694,10	485,97	382,45	320,76	200,54
20 000	1760,90	925,47	647,96	509,93	427,68	267,39
25 000	2201,13	1156,83	809,94	637,41	534,60	334,23
30 000	2641,35	1388,20	971,93	764,89	641,52	401,08
35 000	3081,58	1619,56	1133,92	892,37	748,44	467,93
40 000	3521,80	1850,93	1295,91	1019,85	855,36	534,77
45 000	3962,03	2082,29	1457,90	1147,33	962,28	601,62
50 000	4402,25	2313,66	1619,88	1274,81	1069,20	668,46
60 000	5282,70	2776,39	1943,86	1529,77	1283,03	802,16
70 000	6163,15	3239,12	2267,84	1784,73	1496,87	935,85
80 000	7043,60	3701,85	2591,81	2039,69	1710,71	1069,54
90 000	7924,05	4164,58	2915,79	2294,65	1924,55	1203,23
100 000	8804,50	4627,31	3239,76	2549,61	2138,39	1336,92

48

Required monthly payment to refund a mortgage loan — 10½%

Amount	terms of loan (in years)					
	15	20	25	30	35	40
500	5,46	4,92	4,65	4,50	4,41	4,36
1 000	10,92	9,84	9,29	8,99	8,81	8,71
2 000	21,84	19,67	18,57	17,97	17,62	17,42
3 000	32,75	29,51	27,85	26,95	26,43	26,13
4 000	43,67	39,34	37,14	35,93	35,24	34,84
5 000	54,59	49,18	46,42	44,91	44,05	43,55
6 000	65,50	59,01	55,70	53,89	52,86	52,26
7 000	76,42	68,85	64,99	62,87	61,67	60,97
8 000	87,34	78,68	74,27	71,86	70,48	69,68
9 000	98,25	88,52	83,55	80,84	79,29	78,39
10 000	109,17	98,35	92,84	89,82	88,10	87,10
15 000	163,75	147,53	139,25	134,73	132,15	130,65
20 000	218,33	196,70	185,67	179,63	176,20	174,20
25 000	272,92	245,87	232,09	224,54	220,25	217,75
30 000	327,50	295,05	278,50	269,45	264,29	261,30
35 000	382,08	344,22	324,92	314,35	308,34	304,85
40 000	436,66	393,39	371,34	359,26	352,39	348,40
45 000	491,24	442,57	417,75	404,17	396,44	391,95
50 000	545,83	491,74	464,17	449,08	440,49	435,50
60 000	654,99	590,09	557,00	538,89	528,58	522,59
70 000	764,15	688,44	649,84	628,70	616,68	609,69
80 000	873,32	786,78	742,67	718,52	704,78	696,79
90 000	982,48	885,13	835,50	808,33	792,87	783,89
100 000	1091,65	983,48	928,33	898,15	880,97	870,99

Required monthly payment to refund a mortgage loan

terms of loan (in years)

Amount	1	2	3	4	5	10
500	44,08	23,20	16,26	12,81	10,76	6,76
1 000	88,16	46,39	32,52	25,62	21,51	13,51
2 000	176,32	92,77	65,03	51,23	43,01	27,01
3 000	264,47	139,16	97,54	76,84	64,51	40,51
4 000	352,63	185,54	130,05	102,45	86,01	54,02
5 000	440,79	231,92	162,56	128,06	107,52	67,52
6 000	528,94	278,31	195,07	153,67	129,02	81,02
7 000	617,10	324,69	227,58	179,29	150,52	94,53
8 000	705,26	371,08	260,09	204,90	172,02	108,03
9 000	793,41	417,46	292,60	230,51	193,53	121,53
10 000	881,57	463,84	325,11	256,12	215,03	135,03
15 000	1322,35	695,76	487,66	384,18	322,54	202,55
20 000	1763,13	927,68	650,21	512,24	430,05	270,06
25 000	2203,92	1159,60	812,76	640,29	537,56	337,58
30 000	2644,70	1391,52	975,32	768,35	645,07	405,09
35 000	3085,48	1623,44	1137,87	896,41	752,58	472,61
40 000	3526,26	1855,36	1300,42	1024,47	860,10	540,12
45 000	3967,05	2087,28	1462,97	1152,52	967,61	607,64
50 000	4407,83	2319,20	1625,52	1280,58	1075,12	675,15
60 000	5289,39	2783,04	1950,63	1536,70	1290,14	810,18
70 000	6170,96	3246,87	2275,73	1792,81	1505,16	945,21
80 000	7052,52	3710,71	2600,84	2048,93	1720,19	1080,24
90 000	7934,09	4174,55	2925,94	2305,04	1935,21	1215,27
100 000	8815,65	4638,39	3251,04	2561,16	2150,23	1350,30

Required monthly payment to refund a mortgage loan 10¾%

Amount	terms of loan (in years)					
	15	20	25	30	35	40
500	5,54	5,00	4,73	4,59	4,50	4,45
1 000	11,07	10,00	9,46	9,17	9,00	8,90
2 000	22,13	20,00	18,91	18,33	17,99	17,80
3 000	33,20	29,99	28,37	27,49	26,99	26,70
4 000	44,26	39,99	37,82	36,65	35,98	35,60
5 000	55,33	49,98	47,27	45,81	44,98	44,50
6 000	66,39	59,98	56,73	54,97	53,97	53,40
7 000	77,46	69,97	66,18	64,13	62,97	62,30
8 000	88,52	79,97	75,64	73,29	71,96	71,21
9 000	99,59	89,96	85,09	82,45	80,95	80,10
10 000	110,65	99,96	94,54	91,61	89,95	89,00
15 000	165,97	149,93	141,81	137,41	134,92	133,49
20 000	221,29	199,91	189,08	183,21	179,89	177,99
25 000	276,62	249,88	236,35	229,01	224,86	222,48
30 000	331,94	299,86	283,62	274,81	269,84	266,98
35 000	387,26	349,83	330,89	320,61	314,81	311,47
40 000	442,58	399,81	378,16	366,41	359,78	355,97
45 000	497,91	449,79	425,43	412,21	404,75	400,46
50 000	553,23	499,76	472,70	458,01	449,72	444,96
60 000	663,87	599,71	567,24	549,61	539,67	533,95
70 000	774,52	699,66	661,78	641,21	629,61	622,94
80 000	885,16	799,62	756,31	732,31	719,56	711,93
90 000	995,81	899,57	850,85	824,41	809,50	800,92
100 000	1106,45	999,52	945,39	916,01	899,44	889,91

11% Required monthly payment to refund a mortgage loan

Amount	terms of loan (in years)					
	1	2	3	4	5	10
500	44,14	23,25	16,32	12,87	10,82	6,82
1 000	88,27	46,50	32,63	25,73	21,63	13,64
2 000	176,54	92,99	65,25	51,46	43,25	27,28
3 000	264,81	139,49	97,87	77,19	64,87	40,92
4 000	353,08	185,98	130,50	102,91	86,49	54,55
5 000	441,34	232,48	163,12	128,64	108,11	68,19
6 000	529,61	278,97	195,74	154,37	129,73	81,83
7 000	617,88	325,47	228,37	180,10	151,35	95,47
8 000	706,15	371,96	260,99	205,82	172,97	109,10
9 000	794,42	418,46	293,61	231,55	194,59	122,74
10 000	882,68	464,95	326,24	257,28	216,21	136,38
15 000	1324,02	697,43	489,35	385,91	324,32	204,56
20 000	1765,36	929,90	652,47	514,55	432,42	272,75
25 000	2206,70	1162,37	815,59	643,19	540,53	340,94
30 000	2648,04	1394,85	978,70	771,82	648,63	409,12
35 000	3089,38	1627,32	1141,82	900,40	756,74	477,31
40 000	3530,72	1859,79	1304,94	1029,09	864,84	545,50
45 000	3972,06	2092,27	1468,05	1157,73	972,95	613,68
50 000	4413,40	2324,74	1631,17	1286,37	1081,05	681,87
60 000	5296,08	2789,69	1957,40	1543,64	1297,26	818,24
70 000	6178,76	3254,63	2283,64	1800,91	1513,47	954,62
80 000	7061,44	3719,58	2609,87	2058,18	1729,68	1090,99
90 000	7944,12	4184,53	2936,10	2315,46	1945,89	1227,36
100 000	8826,80	4649,47	3262,34	2572,73	2162,10	1363,73

Amount	terms of loan (in years)					
	15	20	25	30	35	40
500	5,61	5,08	4,82	4,67	4,59	4,55
1 000	11,22	10,16	9,63	9,34	9,18	9,09
2 000	22,43	20,32	19,26	18,68	18,36	18,18
3 000	33,64	30,47	28,88	28,02	27,54	27,27
4 000	44,86	40,63	38,51	37,36	36,72	36,36
5 000	56,07	50,79	48,13	46,70	45,90	45,45
6 000	67,28	60,94	57,76	56,04	55,08	54,54
7 000	78,50	71,10	67,38	65,38	64,26	63,63
8 000	89,71	81,26	77,01	74,72	73,44	72,72
9 000	100,92	91,41	86,63	84,06	82,62	81,80
10 000	112,14	101,57	96,26	93,40	91,80	90,89
15 000	168,20	152,35	144,38	140,10	137,70	136,34
20 000	224,27	203,13	192,51	186,79	183,60	181,78
25 000	280,34	253,91	240,64	233,49	229,50	227,22
30 000	336,40	304,70	288,76	280,19	275,40	272,67
35 000	392,47	355,48	336,89	326,88	321,30	318,11
40 000	448,54	406,26	385,02	373,58	367,19	363,56
45 000	504,60	457,04	433,14	420,28	413,09	409,00
50 000	560,67	507,82	481,27	466,97	458,99	454,44
60 000	672,80	609,39	577,52	560,37	550,79	545,33
70 000	784,93	710,95	673,78	653,76	642,59	636,22
80 000	897,07	812,52	770,03	747,16	734,38	727,11
90 000	1009,20	914,08	866,28	840,55	826,18	818,00
100 000	1121,33	1015,64	962,53	933,94	917,98	908,88

terms of loan (in years)

Amount	1	2	3	4	5	10
500	44,19	23,31	16,37	12,93	10,87	6,89
1 000	88,38	46,61	32,74	25,85	21,74	13,78
2 000	176,76	93,22	65,48	51,69	43,48	27,55
3 000	265,14	139,82	98,21	77,53	65,22	41,32
4 000	353,52	186,43	130,95	103,38	89,96	55,09
5 000	441,90	233,03	163,69	129,22	108,70	68,87
6 000	530,28	279,64	196,42	155,06	130,44	82,64
7 000	618,66	326,24	229,16	180,91	152,18	96,41
8 000	707,04	372,85	261,90	206,75	173,92	110,18
9 000	795,42	419,45	294,63	232,59	195,66	123,95
10 000	883,80	466,06	327,37	258,44	217,40	137,73
15 000	1325,70	699,09	491,05	387,65	326,10	206,59
20 000	1767,59	932,12	654,73	516,87	434,80	275,45
25 000	2209,49	1165,14	818,41	646,08	543,50	344,31
30 000	2651,39	1398,17	982,10	775,30	652,20	413,17
35 000	3093,28	1631,20	1145,98	904,51	760,90	482,03
40 000	3535,18	1864,23	1309,46	1033,73	869,60	550,89
45 000	3977,08	2097,25	1473,14	1162,95	978,30	619,75
50 000	4418,97	2330,28	1636,82	1292,16	1087,00	688,61
60 000	5302,77	2796,34	1964,19	1550,59	1304,40	826,34
70 000	6186,56	3262,39	2291,55	1809,02	1521,80	964,06
80 000	7070,35	3728,45	2618,91	2067,45	1739,20	1101,78
90 000	7954,15	4194,50	2946,28	2325,89	1956,60	1239,50
100 000	8837,94	4660,56	3273,64	2584,32	2174,00	1377,22

Required monthly payment to refund a mortgage loan 11¼%

terms of loan (in years)

Amount	15	20	25	30	35	40
500	5,69	5,16	4,90	4.76	4,69	4,64
1 000	11,37	10,32	9,80	9,52	9,37	9,28
2 000	22,73	20,64	19,60	19,04	18,74	18,56
3 000	34,09	30,96	29,40	28,56	28,10	27,84
4 000	45,46	41,28	39,20	38,08	37,47	37,12
5 000	56,82	51,60	48,99	47,60	46,83	46,40
6 000	68.18	61,92	58,79	57,12	56,20	55,68
7 000	79,55	72,23	68,59	66,64	65,56	64,96
8 000	90,91	82,55	78,39	76,16	74,93	74,24
9 000	102,27	92,87	88,18	85,68	84,30	83,52
10 000	113,63	103,19	97,98	95,20	93,66	92,79
15 000	170,45	154,78	146,97	142,80	140,49	139,19
20 000	227,26	206,38	195,96	190,39	187,32	185,58
25 000	284,08	257,97	244,94	237,99	234,15	231,98
30 000	340,89	309,56	293,93	285,59	280,98	278,37
35 000	397,71	361,15	342,92	333,19	327,80	324,77
40 000	454,52	412,75	391,91	380,78	374,63	371,16
45 000	511,33	464,34	440,89	428,38	421,46	417,56
50 000	568,15	515,93	489,88	475,98	468,29	463,95
60 000	681,78	619,12	587,86	571,17	561,95	556,74
70 000	795,41	722,30	685,83	666,37	655,60	649,53
80 000	909,03	825,49	783,81	761,56	749,26	742,32
90 000	1022,66	928,67	881,78	856,76	842,92	835,11
100 000	1136,29	1031,86	979,76	951,95	936,58	927,90

11½% Required monthly payment to refund a mortgage loan

Amount	terms of loan (in years)					
	1	2	3	4	5	10
500	44,25	23,36	16,43	12,98	10,93	6,96
1 000	88,50	46,72	32,85	25,96	21,86	13,91
2 000	176,99	93,44	65,70	51,92	43,72	27,82
3 000	265,48	140,15	98,55	77,88	65,58	41,73
4 000	353,97	186,87	131,40	103,84	87,44	55,64
5 000	442,46	233,59	164,25	129,80	109,30	69,54
6 000	530,95	280,30	197,10	155,76	131,16	83,45
7 000	619,44	327,02	229,95	181,72	153,02	97,36
8 000	707,93	373,74	262,80	207,68	174,88	111,27
9 000	796,42	420,45	295,65	233,64	196,74	125,17
10 000	884,91	467,17	328,50	259,60	218,60	139,08
15 000	1327,37	700,75	492,75	389,39	327,89	208,62
20 000	1769,82	934,33	657,00	519,19	437,19	278,16
25 000	2212,27	1167,92	821,24	648,99	546,48	347,70
30 000	2654,73	1401,50	985,49	778,78	655,78	417,24
35 000	3097,18	1635,08	1149,74	908,56	765,08	486,77
40 000	3539,63	1868,66	1313,99	1038,37	874,37	556,31
45 000	3982,09	2102,25	1478,23	1168,17	983,67	625,85
50 000	4424,54	2335,83	1642,48	1297,97	1092,96	695,39
60 000	5309,45	2802,99	1970,98	1557,56	1311,56	834,47
70 000	6194,36	3270,16	2299,47	1817,15	1530,15	973,54
80 000	7079,26	3737,32	2627,97	2076,74	1748,74	1112,62
90 000	7964,17	4204,49	2956,46	2336,33	1967,33	1251,70
100 000	8849,08	4671,65	3284,96	2595,93	2185,92	1390,77

Required monthly payment to refund a mortgage loan 11½%

terms of loan (in years)

Amount	15	20	25	30	35	40
500	5,76	5,25	4,99	4,86	4,78	4,74
1 000	11,52	10,49	9,98	9,71	9,56	9,47
2 000	23,03	20,97	19,95	19,41	19,11	18,94
3 000	34,54	31,45	29,92	29,11	28,66	28,41
4 000	46,06	41,93	39,89	38,81	38,21	37,88
5 000	57,57	52,41	49,86	48,51	47,77	47,35
6 000	69,08	62,89	59,83	58,21	57,32	56,82
7 000	80.60	73,38	69,80	67,91	66,87	66,29
8 000	92,11	83,86	79,77	77,61	76,42	75,76
9 000	103,62	94,34	89,74	87,31	85,98	85,23
10 000	115,14	104,82	99,71	97,01	95,53	94,70
15 000	172,70	157,23	149,56	145,51	143,29	142,05
20 000	230,27	209,63	199,42	194,01	191,05	189,40
25 000	287,84	262,04	249,27	242,51	238,81	236,75
30 000	345,40	314,45	299,12	291,01	286,57	284,09
35 000	402,97	366,86	348,98	339,52	334,33	331,44
40 000	460,53	419,26	398,83	388,02	382,09	378,79
45 000	518,10	471,67	448,68	436,52	429,86	426,14
50 000	575,67	524,08	498,54	485,02	477,62	473,49
60 000	690,80	628,89	598,24	582,02	573,14	568,18
70 000	805,93	733,71	697,95	679,03	668,66	662,88
80 000	921,06	838,52	797,65	776,03	764,18	757,57
90 000	1036,19	943,34	897,36	873,03	859,71	852,27
100 000	1151,33	1048,15	997,07	970,04	955,23	946,97

11¾% Required monthly payment to refund a mortgage loan

Amount	1	2	3	4	5	10
	\multicolumn{6}{c}{terms of loan (in years)}					
500	44,31	23,42	16,49	13,04	10,99	7,03
1 000	88,61	46,83	32,97	26,08	21,98	14,05
2 000	177,21	93,66	65,93	52,16	43,96	28,09
3 000	265,81	140,49	98,89	78,23	65,94	42,14
4 000	354,41	187,31	131,86	104,31	87,92	56,18
5 000	443,02	234,14	164,82	130,38	109,90	70,22
6 000	531,62	280,97	197,78	156,46	131,88	84,27
7 000	620,22	327,80	230,74	182,53	153,86	98,31
8 000	708,82	374,62	263,71	208,61	175,83	112,35
9 000	797,42	421,45	296,67	234,68	197,81	126,40
10 000	886,03	468,28	329,63	260,76	219,79	140,44
15 000	1329,04	702,42	494,45	391,14	329,69	210,66
20 000	1772,05	936,55	659,26	521,51	439,58	280,88
25 000	2215,06	1170,69	824,08	651,89	549,47	351,10
30 000	2658,07	1404,83	988,89	782,27	659,37	421,32
35 000	3101,08	1638,96	1153,70	912,65	769,26	491,53
40 000	3544,09	1873,10	1318,52	1043,02	879,15	561,75
45 000	3987,10	2107,24	1483,33	1173,40	989,05	631,97
50 000	4430,11	2341,38	1648,15	1303,78	1098,94	702,19
60 000	5316,13	2809,65	1977,77	1564,53	1318,73	842,63
70 000	6202,15	3277,92	2307,40	1825,29	1538,51	983,06
80 000	7088,17	3746,20	2637,03	2086,04	1758,30	1123,50
90 000	7974,19	4214,47	2966,66	2346,80	1978,09	1263,94
100 000	8860,22	4682,75	3296,29	2607,55	2197,87	1404,37

Required monthly payment to refund a mortgage loan 11¾%

Amount	terms of loan (in years)					
	15	20	25	30	35	40
500	5,84	5,33	5,08	4,95	4,87	4,84
1 000	11,67	10,65	10,15	9,89	9,74	9,67
2 000	23,33	21,30	20,29	19,77	19,48	19,33
3 000	35,00	31,94	30,44	29,65	29,22	28,99
4 000	46,66	42,59	40,58	39,53	38,96	38,65
5 000	58,33	53,23	50,73	49,41	48,70	48,31
6 000	69,99	63,88	60,87	59,30	58,44	57,97
7 000	81,65	74,52	71,02	69,18	68,18	67,63
8 000	93,32	85,17	81,16	79,06	77,92	77,29
9 000	104,98	95,81	91,30	88,94	87,66	86,95
10 000	116,65	106,46	101,45	98,82	97,40	96,61
15 000	174,97	159,68	152,17	148,23	146,09	144,91
20 000	233,29	212,91	202,89	197,64	194,79	193,22
25 000	291,61	266,14	253,62	247,05	243,49	241,52
30 000	349,93	319,36	304,34	296,46	292,18	289,82
35 000	408,25	372,59	355,06	345,87	340,88	338,13
40 000	466,58	425,81	405,78	395,28	389,58	386,43
45 000	524,90	479,04	456,50	444,68	438,27	434,73
50 000	583,22	532,27	507,23	494,09	486,97	483,03
60 000	699,86	638,72	608,67	592,91	584,36	579,64
70 000	816,50	745,17	710,12	691,73	681,76	676,25
80 000	933,15	851,62	811,56	790,55	779,15	772,85
90 000	1049,79	958,07	913,00	889,36	876,54	869,46
100 000	1166,43	1064,53	1014,45	988,18	973,93	966,06

12%

Required monthly payment to refund a mortgage loan

terms of loan (in years)

Amount	1	2	3	4	5	10
500	44,36	23,47	16,54	13,10	11,05	7,10
1 000	88,72	46,94	33,08	26,20	22,10	14,19
2 000	177,43	93,88	66,16	52,39	44,20	28,37
3 000	266,15	140,82	99,23	78,58	66,30	42,55
4 000	354,86	187,76	132,31	104,77	88,40	56,73
5 000	443,57	234,70	165,39	130,96	110,50	70,91
6 000	532,29	281,64	198,46	157,16	132,60	85,09
7 000	621,00	328,57	231,54	183,35	154,69	99,27
8 000	709,71	375,51	264,61	209,54	176,79	113,45
9 000	798,43	422,45	297,69	235,73	198,89	127,63
10 000	887,14	469,39	330,77	261,92	220,99	141,81
15 000	1330,71	704,08	496,15	392,88	331,48	212,71
20 000	1774,27	938,77	661,53	523,84	441,97	283,61
25 000	2217,84	1173,47	826,91	654,80	552,47	354,51
30 000	2661,41	1408,16	992,29	785,76	662,96	425,41
35 000	3104,98	1642,85	1157,67	916,72	773,45	496,31
40 000	3548,54	1877,54	1323,05	1047,68	883,94	567,22
45 000	3992,11	2112,23	1488,44	1178,64	994,44	638,12
50 000	4435,68	2346,93	1653,82	1309,60	1104,93	709,02
60 000	5322,81	2816,31	1984,58	1571,52	1325,91	850,82
70 000	6209,95	3285,69	2315,34	1833,44	1546,90	992,62
80 000	7097,08	3755,08	2646,10	2095,36	1767,88	1134,43
90 000	7984,21	4224,46	2976,87	2357,28	1988,87	1276,23
100 000	8871,35	4693,85	3307,63	2619,20	2209,85	1418,03

Required monthly payment to refund a mortgage loan   **12%**

terms of loan (in years)

Amount	15	20	25	30	35	40
500	5,91	5,41	5,16	5,04	4,97	4,93
1 000	11,82	10,81	10,32	10,07	9,93	9,86
2 000	23,64	21,62	20,64	20,13	19,86	19,71
3 000	35,45	32,43	30,96	30,20	29,79	29,56
4 000	47,27	43,24	41,28	40,26	39,71	39,41
5 000	59,09	54,05	51,60	50,32	49,64	49,26
6 000	70,90	64,86	61,92	60,39	59,57	59,12
7 000	82,72	75,67	72,24	70,45	69,49	68,97
8 000	94,53	86,48	82,56	80,52	79,42	78,82
9 000	106,35	97,29	92,88	90,58	89,35	88,67
10 000	118,17	108,10	103,19	100,64	99,27	98,52
15 000	177,25	162,15	154,79	150,96	148,91	147,78
20 000	236,33	216,20	206,38	201,28	198,54	197,04
25 000	295,41	270,25	257,98	251,60	248,18	246,30
30 000	354,49	324,30	309,57	301,92	297,81	295,56
35 000	413,57	378,35	361,17	352,24	347,44	344,82
40 000	472,65	432,39	412,76	402,56	397,08	394,08
45 000	531,73	486,44	464,36	452,88	446,71	443,34
50 000	590,81	540,49	515,95	503,20	496,35	492,60
60 000	708,97	648,59	619,14	603,84	595,61	591,12
70 000	827,13	756,69	722,33	704,48	694,88	689,64
80 000	945,29	864,78	825,52	805,11	794,15	788,16
90 000	1063,45	972,88	928,71	905,75	893,42	886,68
100 000	1181,61	1080,98	1031,90	1006,39	992,69	985,20

12¼%   Required monthly payment to refund a mortgage loan

Amount	terms of loan (in years)					
	1	2	3	4	5	10
500	44,42	23,53	16,60	13,16	11,11	7,16
1 000	88,83	47,05	33,19	26,31	22,22	14,32
2 000	177,65	94,10	66,38	52,62	44,44	28,64
3 000	266,48	141,15	99,57	78,93	66,66	42,96
4 000	355,30	188,20	132,76	105,24	88,88	57,27
5 000	444,13	235,25	165,95	131,55	111,10	71,59
6 000	532,95	282,30	199,14	157,86	133,32	85,91
7 000	621,78	329,35	232,33	184,17	155,53	100,23
8 000	710,60	376,40	265,52	210,47	177,75	114,54
9 000	799,43	423,45	298,71	236,78	199,97	128,86
10 000	888,25	470,50	331,90	263,09	222,19	143,18
15 000	1332,38	705,75	497,85	394,63	333,28	214,77
20 000	1776,50	940,99	663,80	526,18	444,37	286,35
25 000	2220,62	1176,24	829,75	657,72	555,47	357,94
30 000	2664,75	1411,49	995,70	789,26	666,56	429,53
35 000	3108,87	1646,74	1161,65	920,81	777,65	501,11
40 000	3552,99	1881,98	1327,60	1052,35	888,74	572,70
45 000	3997,12	2117,23	1493,54	1183,89	999,84	644,29
50 000	4441,24	2352,48	1659,49	1315,43	1110,93	715,87
60 000	5329,49	2822,97	1991,39	1578,52	1333,11	859,05
70 000	6217,74	3293,47	2323,29	1841,61	1555,30	1002,22
80 000	7105,98	3763,96	2655,19	2104,69	1777,48	1145,40
90 000	7994,23	4234,46	2987,08	2367,78	1999,67	1288,57
100 000	8882,48	4704,95	3318,98	2630,86	2221,85	1431,74

Required monthly payment to refund a mortgage loan 12¼%

terms of loan (in years)

Amount	15	20	25	30	35	40
500	5,99	5,49	5,25	5,13	5,06	5,03
1 000	11,97	10,98	10,50	10,25	10,12	10,05
2 000	23,94	21,96	20,99	20,50	20,23	20,09
3 000	35,91	32,93	31,49	30,74	30,35	30,14
4 000	47,88	43,91	41,98	40,99	40,46	40,18
5 000	59,85	54,88	52,48	51,24	50,58	50,22
6 000	71,82	65,86	62,97	61,48	60,69	60,27
7 000	83,79	76,83	73,46	71,73	70,81	70,31
8 000	95,75	87,81	83,96	81,98	80,92	80,35
9 000	107,72	98,78	94,45	92,22	91,04	90,40
10 000	119,69	109,76	104,95	102,47	101,15	100,44
15 000	179,53	164,63	157,42	153,70	151,73	150,66
20 000	239,38	219,51	209,89	204,94	202,30	200,88
25 000	299,22	274,38	262,36	256,17	252,88	251,09
30 000	359,06	329,26	314,83	307,40	303,45	301,31
35 000	418,91	384,13	367,30	358,63	354,02	351,53
40 000	478,75	439,01	419,78	409,87	404,60	401,75
45 000	538,59	493,88	472,25	461,10	455,17	451,96
50 000	598,44	548,76	524,72	512,33	505,75	502,18
60 000	718,12	658,51	629,66	614,80	606,89	602,62
70 000	837,81	768,26	734,60	717,26	708,04	703,05
80 000	957,49	878,01	839,55	819,73	809,19	803,49
90 000	1077,18	987,76	944,49	922,20	910,34	903,92
100 000	1196,87	1097,51	1049,43	1024,66	1011,49	1004,36

12½% Required monthly payment to refund a mortgage loan

terms of loan (in years)

Amount	1	2	3	4	5	10
500	44,47	23,59	16,66	13,22	11,17	7,23
1 000	88,94	47,17	33,31	26,43	22,34	14,46
2 000	177,88	94,33	66,61	52,86	44,68	28,92
3 000	266,81	141,49	99,92	79,28	67,02	43,37
4 000	355,75	188,65	133,22	105,71	89,36	57,83
5 000	444,69	235,81	166,52	132,13	111,70	72,28
6 000	533,62	282,97	199,83	158,56	134,04	86,74
7 000	622,56	330,13	233,13	184,98	156,38	101,19
8 000	711,49	377,29	266,43	211,41	178,71	115,65
9 000	800,43	424,45	299,74	237,83	201,05	130,10
10 000	889,37	471,61	333,04	264,26	223,39	144,56
15 000	1334,05	707,41	499,56	396,39	335,09	216,83
20 000	1778,73	943,22	666,07	528,51	446,70	289,11
25 000	2223,41	1179,02	832,59	660,64	558,47	361,38
30 000	2668,09	1414,82	999,11	792,77	670,17	433,66
35 000	3112,77	1650,62	1165,62	924,90	781,86	505,93
40 000	3557,45	1886,43	1332,14	1057,02	893,55	578,21
45 000	4002,13	2122,23	1498,66	1189,15	1005,25	650,48
50 000	4446,81	2358,03	1665,18	1321,28	1116,94	722,76
60 000	5336,17	2829,64	1998,21	1585,53	1340,33	867,31
70 000	6225,53	3301,24	2331,24	1849,79	1563,72	1011,86
80 000	7114,89	3772,85	2664,28	2114,04	1787,10	1156,41
90 000	8004,25	4244,46	2997,31	2378,29	2010,49	1300,96
100 000	8893,61	4716,06	3330,35	2642,55	2233,88	1445,31

Required monthly payment to refund a mortgage loan 12½%

Amount	terms of loan (in years)					
	15	20	25	30	35	40
500	6,07	5,58	5,34	5,22	5,16	5,12
1 000	12,13	11,15	10,68	10,43	10,31	10,24
2 000	24,25	22,29	21,35	20,86	20,61	20,48
3 000	36,37	33,43	32,02	31,29	30,91	30,71
4 000	48,49	44,57	42,69	41,72	41,22	40,95
5 000	60,61	55,71	53,36	52,15	51,52	51,18
6 000	72,74	66,85	64,03	62,58	61,82	61,42
7 000	84,86	77,99	74,70	73,01	72,13	71,65
8 000	96,98	89,13	85,37	83,44	82,43	81,89
9 000	109,10	100,27	96,04	93,87	92,73	92,12
10 000	121,22	111,42	106,71	104,30	103,04	102,36
15 000	181,83	167,12	160,06	156,45	154,55	153,54
20 000	242,44	222,83	213,41	208,60	206,07	204,71
25 000	303,05	278,53	266,76	260,75	257,59	255,89
30 000	363,66	334,24	320,11	312,90	309,10	307,07
35 000	424,27	389,94	373,46	365,05	360,62	358,25
40 000	484,88	445,65	426,81	417,20	412,13	409,42
45 000	545,49	501,35	480,17	469,35	463,65	460,60
50 000	606,10	557,06	533,52	521,50	515,17	511,78
60 000	727,32	668,47	640,22	625,79	618,20	614,13
70 000	848,53	779,88	746,92	730,09	721,23	716,49
80 000	969,75	891,29	853,62	834,39	824,26	818,84
90 000	1090,97	1002,70	960,33	938,69	927,29	921,20
100 000	1212,19	1114,11	1067,03	1042,99	1030,33	1023,55

12¾% Required monthly payment to refund a mortgage loan

terms of loan (in years)

Amount	1	2	3	4	5	10
500	44,53	23,64	16,71	13,28	11,23	7,30
1 000	89,05	47,28	33,42	26,55	22,46	14,60
2 000	178,10	94,55	66,84	53,09	44,92	29,19
3 000	267,15	141,82	100,26	79,63	67,38	43,78
4 000	356,19	189,09	133,67	106,17	89,84	58,38
5 000	445,24	236,36	167,09	132,72	112,30	72,97
6 000	534,29	283,64	200,51	159,26	134,76	87,56
7 000	623,34	330,91	233,93	185,80	157,22	102,16
8 000	712,38	378,18	267,34	212,34	179,68	116,75
9 000	801,43	425,45	300,76	238,89	202,14	131,34
10 000	890,48	472,72	334,18	265,43	224,60	145,94
15 000	1335,71	709,08	501,26	398,14	336,89	218,90
20 000	1780,95	945,44	668,35	530,85	449,19	291,87
25 000	2226,19	1181,80	835,43	663,57	561,49	364,84
30 000	2671,42	1418,16	1002,52	796,28	673,78	437,80
35 000	3116,66	1654,51	1169,61	928,99	786,08	510,77
40 000	3561,89	1890,87	1336,69	1061,70	898,38	583,73
45 000	4007,13	2127,23	1503,78	1194,42	1010,67	656,70
50 000	4452,37	2363,59	1670,86	1327,13	1122,97	729,67
60 000	5342,84	2836,31	2005,03	1592,55	1347,56	875,60
70 000	6233,31	3309,02	2339,21	1857,98	1572,15	1021,53
80 000	7123,78	3781,74	2673,38	2123,40	1796,75	1167,46
90 000	8014,26	4254,46	3007,55	2388,83	2021,34	1313,40
100 000	8904,73	4727,17	3341,72	2654,25	2245,93	1459,33

Required monthly payment to refund a mortgage loan 12¾%

Amount	terms of loan (in years)					
	15	20	25	30	35	40
500	6,14	5,66	5,43	5,31	5,25	5,22
1 000	12,28	11,31	10,85	10,62	10,50	10,43
2 000	24,56	22,62	21,70	21,23	20,99	20,86
3 000	36,83	33,93	32,55	31,85	31,48	31,29
4 000	49,11	45,24	43,39	42,46	41,97	41,72
5 000	61,38	56,54	54,24	53,07	52,46	52,14
6 000	73,66	67,85	65,09	63,69	62,96	62,57
7 000	85,94	79,16	75,93	74,30	73,45	73,00
8 000	98,21	90,47	86,78	84,91	83,94	83,43
9 000	110,49	101,78	97,63	95,53	94,43	93,85
10 000	122,76	113,08	108,47	106,14	104,92	104,28
15 000	184,14	169,62	162,71	159,21	157,38	156,42
20 000	245,52	226,16	216,94	212,28	209,84	208,56
25 000	306,90	282,70	271,18	265,35	262,30	260,70
30 000	368,28	339,24	325,41	318,41	314,76	312,83
35 000	429,66	395,78	379,64	371,48	367,22	364,97
40 000	491,04	452,32	433,88	424,55	419,68	417,11
45 000	552,41	508,86	488,11	477,62	472,14	469,25
50 000	613,79	565,40	542,35	530,69	524,60	521,39
60 000	736,55	678,48	650,82	636,82	629,52	625,66
70 000	859,31	791,55	759,28	742,96	734,44	729,94
80 000	982,07	904,63	867,75	849,09	839,36	834,21
90 000	1104,82	1017,71	976,22	955,23	944,28	938,49
100 000	1227,58	1130,79	1084,69	1061,37	1049,20	1042,77

13% Required monthly payment to refund a mortgage loan

Amount	terms of loan (in years)					
	1	2	3	4	5	10
500	44,58	23,70	16,77	13,33	11,30	7,37
1 000	89,16	47,39	33,54	26,66	22,59	14,74
2 000	178,32	94,77	67,07	53,32	45,17	29,47
3 000	267,48	142,15	100,60	79,98	67,75	44,20
4 000	356,64	189,54	134.13	106,64	90,33	58,93
5 000	445,80	236.92	167.66	133,30	112,91	73,66
6 000	534,96	284,30	201,19	159,96	135,49	88,40
7 000	624,11	331,69	234,72	186,62	158,07	103,13
8 000	713,27	379,07	268,25	213,28	180,65	117,86
9 000	802,43	426,45	301,78	239,94	203,23	132,59
10 000	891,59	473,83	335,32	266,60	225,81	147,32
15 000	1337,38	710,75	502,97	399,90	338,71	220,98
20 000	1783,17	947,66	670,63	533,20	451,61	294,64
25 000	2228,97	1184,58	838,28	666,50	564,51	368,30
30 000	2674,76	1421,49	1005,94	799,80	677,41	441,96
35 000	3120,55	1658,41	1173,59	933,09	790,31	515,62
40 000	3566,34	1895,32	1341,25	1066,39	903,21	589,28
45 000	4012,13	2132,23	1508,90	1199,69	1016,11	662,94
50 000	4457,93	2369,15	1676,56	1332,99	1129,01	736,60
60 000	5349,51	2842,98	2011,87	1599,59	1354,81	883,92
70 000	6241,10	3316,81	2347,18	1866,18	1580,61	1031,24
80 000	7132,68	3790,64	2682,49	2132,78	1806,41	1178,56
90 000	8024,26	4264,46	3017,80	2399,38	2032,21	1325,88
100 000	8915,85	4738,29	3353,11	2665,97	2258,01	1473,20

Amount	terms of loan (in years)					
	15	20	25	30	35	40
500	6,22	5,74	5,52	5,40	5,35	5,31
1 000	12,44	11,48	11,03	10,80	10,69	10,62
2 000	24,87	22,96	22,05	21,60	21,37	21,24
3 000	37,30	34,43	33,08	32,40	32,05	31,86
4 000	49,73	45,91	44,10	43,20	42,73	42,48
5 000	62,16	57,38	55,13	53,99	53,41	53,10
6 000	74,59	68,86	66,15	64,79	64,09	63,72
7 000	87,02	80,33	77,17	75,59	74,77	74,34
8 000	99,45	91,81	88,20	86,39	85,45	84,96
9 000	111,88	103,28	99,22	97,19	96,14	95,58
10 000	124,31	114,76	110,25	107,98	106,82	106,20
15 000	186,46	172,13	165,37	161,97	160,22	159,30
20 000	248,61	229,51	220,49	215,96	213,63	212,40
25 000	310,76	286,89	275,61	269,95	267,03	265,50
30 000	372,92	344,26	330,73	323,94	320,44	318,60
35 000	435,07	401,64	385,85	377,93	373,84	371,70
40 000	497,22	459,02	440,97	431,92	427,25	424,80
45 000	559,37	516,39	496,09	485,91	480,66	477,90
50 000	621,52	573,77	551,21	539,90	534,06	531,00
60 000	745,83	688,52	661,45	647,88	640,87	637,20
70 000	870,13	803,28	771,69	755,86	747,68	743,40
80 000	994,43	918,03	881,93	863,84	854,50	849,60
90 000	1118,74	1032,78	992,17	971,81	961,31	955,80
100 000	1243,04	1147,54	1102,41	1079,79	1068,12	1062,00

13¼% Required monthly payment to refund a mortgage loan

Amount	terms of loan (in years)					
	1	2	3	4	5	10
500	44,64	23,75	16,83	13,39	11,36	7,44
1 000	89,27	47,50	33,65	26,78	22,71	14,88
2 000	178,54	94,99	67,30	53,56	45,41	29,75
3 000	267,81	142,49	100,94	80,34	68,11	44,62
4 000	357,08	189,98	134,59	107,11	90,81	59,49
5 000	446,35	237,48	168,23	133,89	113,51	74,36
6 000	535,62	284,97	201,88	160,67	136,21	89,23
7 000	624,89	332,46	235,52	187,44	158,91	104,10
8 000	714,16	379,96	269,17	214,22	181,61	118,97
9 000	803,43	427,45	302,81	241,00	204,41	133,85
10 000	892,70	474,95	336,46	267,78	227,02	148,72
15 000	1339,05	712,42	504,68	401,66	340,52	223,07
20 000	1785,40	949,89	672,91	535,55	454,03	297,43
25 000	2231,75	1187,36	841,13	669,43	567,53	371,79
30 000	2678,09	1424,83	1009,36	803,32	681,04	446,14
35 000	3124,44	1662,30	1177,58	937,20	794,54	520,50
40 000	3570,79	1899,77	1345,81	1071,09	908,05	594,85
45 000	4017,14	2137,24	1514,03	1204,97	1021,55	669,21
50 000	4463,49	2374,71	1682,26	1338,86	1135,06	743,57
60 000	5356,18	2849,65	2018,71	1606,63	1362,07	892,28
70 000	6248,88	3324,59	2355,16	1874,40	1589,08	1040,99
80 000	7141,57	3799,53	2691,61	2142,17	1816,09	1189,70
90 000	8034,27	4274,47	3028,06	2409,94	2043,10	1338,41
100 000	8926,97	4749,42	3364,51	2677,71	2270,11	1487,13

Required monthly payment to refund a mortgage loan 13¼%

terms of loan (in years)

Amount	15	20	25	30	35	40
500	6,30	5,83	5,61	5,50	5,44	5,41
1 000	12,59	11,65	11,21	10,99	10,88	10,82
2 000	25,18	23,29	22,41	21,97	21,75	21,63
3 000	37,76	34,94	33,61	32,95	32,62	32,44
4 000	50,35	46,58	44,81	43,94	43,49	43,26
5 000	62,93	58,22	56,01	54,92	54,36	54,07
6 000	75,52	69,87	67,22	65,90	65,23	64,88
7 000	88,10	81,51	78,42	76,88	76,10	75,69
8 000	100,69	93,15	89,62	87,87	86,97	86,51
9 000	113,28	104,80	100,82	98,85	97,84	97,32
10 000	125,86	116,44	112,02	109,83	108,71	108,13
15 000	188,79	174,66	168,03	164,74	163,06	162,19
20 000	251,72	232,87	224,04	219,66	217,42	216,26
25 000	314,65	291,09	280,05	274,57	271,77	270,32
30 000	377,57	349,31	336,06	329,48	326,12	324,38
35 000	440,50	407,53	392,07	384,40	380,48	378,44
40 000	503,43	465,74	448,08	439,31	434,83	432,51
45 000	566,36	523,96	504,09	494,22	489,18	486,57
50 000	629,29	582,18	560,10	549,14	543,53	540,63
60 000	755,14	698,61	672,12	658,96	652,24	648,76
70 000	881,00	815,05	784,14	768,79	760,95	756,88
80 000	1006,86	931,48	896,16	878,62	869,65	865,01
90 000	1132,71	1047,92	1008,18	988,44	978,36	973,13
100 000	1258,57	1164,35	1120,20	1098,27	1087,06	1081,26

71

13½% Required monthly payment to refund a mortgage loan

Amount	terms of loan (in years)					
	1	2	3	4	5	10
500	44,70	23,81	16,88	13,45	11,42	7,51
1 000	89,39	47,61	33,76	26,90	22,83	15,02
2 000	178,77	95,22	67,52	53,79	45,65	30,03
3 000	268,15	142,82	101,28	80,69	68,47	45,04
4 000	357,53	190,43	135,04	107,58	91,29	60,05
5 000	446,91	238,03	168,80	134,48	114,12	75,06
6 000	536,29	285,64	202,56	161,37	136,94	90,07
7 000	625,67	333,24	236,32	188,27	159,76	105,08
8 000	715,05	380,85	270,08	215,16	182,58	120,09
9 000	804,43	428,45	303 84	242,06	205,41	135,10
10 000	893,81	476,06	337,60	268,95	228,23	150,11
15 000	1340,72	714,09	506,39	403,03	342,34	225,17
20 000	1787,62	952,11	675,19	537,90	456,45	300,22
25 000	2234,52	1190,14	843,98	672,37	570,56	375,28
30 000	2681,43	1428,17	1012,18	806,85	684,68	450,33
35 000	3128,33	1666,19	1181,57	941,32	798,79	525,39
40 000	3575,23	1904,22	1350,37	1075,79	912,90	600,44
45 000	4022,14	2142,25	1519,17	1210,27	1027,01	675,50
50 000	4469,04	2380,27	1687,96	1344,74	1141,12	750,55
60 000	5362,85	2856,33	2025,55	1613,69	1369,35	900,66
70 000	6256,66	3332,38	2363,14	1882,63	1597,57	1050,77
80 000	7150,46	3808,44	2700,74	2151,58	1825,80	1200,88
90 000	8044,27	4284,49	3038,33	2420,53	2054,02	1350,99
100 000	8938,08	4760,54	3375,92	2689,47	2282,24	1501,10

Required monthly payment to refund a mortgage loan 13½%

Amount	terms of loan (in years)					
	15	20	25	30	35	40
500	6,38	5,91	5,70	5,59	5,54	5,51
1 000	12,75	11,82	11,39	11,17	11,07	11,01
2 000	25,49	23,63	22,77	22,34	22,13	22,02
3 000	38,23	35,44	34,15	33,51	33,19	33,02
4 000	50,97	47,25	45,53	44,68	44,25	44,03
5 000	63,71	59,07	56,91	55,84	55,31	55,03
6 000	76,45	70,88	68,29	67,01	66,37	66,04
7 000	89,20	82,69	79,67	78,18	77,43	77,04
8 000	101,94	94,50	91,05	89,35	88,49	88,05
9 000	114,68	106,32	102,43	100,52	99,55	99,05
10 000	127,42	118,13	113,81	111,68	110,61	110,06
15 000	191,13	177,19	170,71	167,52	165,91	165,08
20 000	254,84	236,25	227,61	223,36	221,21	220,11
25 000	318,54	295,31	284,51	279,20	276,51	275,14
30 000	382,25	354,37	341,41	335,04	331,82	330,16
35 000	445,96	413,43	398,32	390,88	387,12	385,19
40 000	509,67	472,50	455,22	446,72	442,42	440,21
45 000	573,37	531,56	512,12	502,56	497,72	495,24
50 000	637,08	590,62	569,02	558,40	553,02	550,27
60 000	764,50	708,74	682,82	670,07	663,63	660,32
70 000	891,91	826,86	796,63	781,75	774,23	770,37
80 000	1019,33	944,99	910,43	893,43	884,83	880,42
90 000	1146,74	1063,11	1024,23	1005,11	995,44	990,48
100 000	1274,16	1181,23	1138,04	1116,79	1106,04	1100,53

13¾% Required monthly payment to refund a mortgage loan

Amount	terms of loan (in years)					
	1	2	3	4	5	10
500	44,75	23,86	16,94	13,51	11,48	7,58
1 000	89,50	47,72	33,88	27,02	22,95	15,16
2 000	178,99	95,44	67,75	54,03	45,89	30,31
3 000	268,48	143,16	101,63	81,04	68,84	45,46
4 000	357,97	190,87	135,50	108,05	91,78	60,61
5 000	447,46	238,59	169,37	135,07	114,72	75,76
6 000	536,96	286,31	203,25	162,08	137,67	90,91
7 000	626,45	334,02	237,12	189,09	160,61	106,06
8 000	715,94	381,74	270,99	216,10	183,56	121,21
9 000	805,43	429,46	304,87	243,12	206,50	136,37
10 000	894,92	477,17	338,74	270,13	229,44	151,52
15 000	1342,38	715,76	508,11	405,19	344,16	227,27
20 000	1789,84	954,34	677,47	540,25	458,88	303,03
25 000	2237,30	1192,92	846,84	675,32	573,60	378,79
30 000	2684,76	1431,51	1016,21	810,38	688,32	454,54
35 000	3132,22	1670,09	1185,57	945,44	803,04	530,30
40 000	3579,68	1908,67	1354,94	1080,50	917,76	606,05
45 000	4027,14	2147,26	1524,31	1215,57	1032,48	681,81
50 000	4474,60	2385,84	1693,67	1350,63	1147,20	757,57
60 000	5369,52	2863,01	2032,41	1620,75	1376,64	909,08
70 000	6264,43	3340,17	2371,14	1890,88	1606,08	1060,59
80 000	7159,35	3817,34	2709,87	2161,00	1835,52	1212,10
90 000	8054,27	4294,51	3048,61	2431,13	2064,96	1363,62
100 000	8949,19	4771,67	3387,34	2701,25	2294,40	1515,13

Required monthly payment to refund a mortgage loan 13¾%

Amount	terms of loan (in years)					
	15	20	25	30	35	40
500	6,45	6,00	5,78	5,68	5,63	5,60
1 000	12,90	11,99	11,56	11,36	11,26	11,20
2 000	25,80	23,97	23,12	22,71	22,51	22,40
3 000	38,70	35,95	34,68	34,07	33,76	33,60
4 000	51,60	47,93	46,24	45,42	45,01	44,80
5 000	64,50	59,91	57,80	56,77	56,26	56,00
6 000	77,39	71,90	69,36	68,13	67,51	67,19
7 000	90,29	83,88	80,92	79,48	78,76	78,39
8 000	103,19	95,86	92,48	90,83	90,01	89,59
9 000	116,09	107,84	104,04	102,19	101,26	100,79
10 000	128,99	119,82	115,60	113,54	112,51	111,99
15 000	193,48	179,73	173,39	170,31	168,76	167,98
20 000	257,97	239,64	231,19	227,07	225,01	223,97
25 000	322,46	299,55	288,99	283,84	281,26	279,96
30 000	386,95	359,46	346,78	340,61	337,52	335,95
35 000	451,44	419,36	404,58	397,37	393,77	391,94
40 000	515,93	479,27	462,38	454,14	450,02	447,93
45 000	580,52	539,18	520,17	510,91	506,27	503,92
50 000	644,91	599,09	577,97	567,68	562,52	559,91
60 000	773,89	718,91	693,56	681,21	675,03	671,89
70 000	902,87	838,72	809,15	794,74	787,53	783,87
80 000	1031,85	958,54	924,75	908,28	900,03	895,85
90 000	1160,84	1078,36	1040,34	1021,81	1012,54	1007,83
100 000	1289,82	1198,17	1155,93	1135,35	1125,04	1119,81

14% Required monthly payment to refund a mortgage loan

Amount	terms of loan (in years)					
	1	2	3	4	5	10
500	44,81	23,92	17,00	13,57	11,54	7,65
1 000	89,61	47,83	33,99	27,14	23,07	15,30
2 000	179,21	95,66	67,98	54,27	46,14	30,59
3 000	268,81	143,49	101,97	81,40	69,20	45,88
4 000	358,42	191,32	135,96	108,53	92,27	61,17
5 000	448,02	239,15	169,94	135,66	115,33	76,47
6 000	537,62	286,97	203,93	162,79	138,40	91,76
7 000	627,23	334,80	237,92	189,92	161,46	107,05
8 000	716,83	382,63	271,91	217,05	184,53	122,34
9 000	806,43	430,46	305,89	244,18	207,60	137,63
10 000	896,03	478,29	339,88	271,31	230,66	152,93
15 000	1344,05	717,43	509,82	406,96	345,99	229,39
20 000	1792,06	956,57	679,76	542,61	461,32	305,85
25 000	2240,08	1195,71	849,70	678,26	576,65	382,31
30 000	2688,09	1434,85	1019,64	813,92	691,98	458,77
35 000	3136,11	1673,99	1189,57	949,57	807,30	535,23
40 000	3584,12	1913,13	1359,51	1085,22	922,63	611,69
45 000	4032,14	2152,27	1529,45	1220,87	1037,96	688,15
50 000	4480,15	2391,41	1699,39	1356,52	1153,29	764,61
60 000	5376,18	2869,69	2039,27	1627,83	1383,95	917,53
70 000	6272,21	3347,97	2379,14	1899,13	1614,60	1070,45
80 000	7168,24	3826,25	2719,02	2170,44	1845,26	1223,37
90 000	8064,27	4304,53	3058,90	2441,74	2075,92	1376,29
100 000	8960,30	4782,81	3398,77	2713,04	2306,57	1529,21

Required monthly payment to refund a mortgage loan

14%

Amount	terms of loan (in years)					
	15	20	25	30	35	40
500	6,53	6,08	5,87	5,77	5,73	5,70
1 000	13,06	12,16	11,74	11,54	11,45	11,40
2 000	26,12	24,31	23,48	23,08	22,89	22,79
3 000	39,17	36,46	35,22	34,62	34,33	34,18
4 000	52,23	48,61	46,96	46,16	45,77	45,57
5 000	65,28	60,76	58,70	57,70	57,21	56,96
6 000	78,34	72,92	70,44	69,24	68,65	68,35
7 000	91,39	85,07	82,18	80,78	80,09	79,74
8 000	104,45	97,22	93,92	92,32	91,53	91,13
9 000	117,50	109,37	105,65	103,86	102,97	102,52
10 000	130,56	121,52	117,39	115,40	114,41	113,92
15 000	195,83	182,28	176,09	173,10	171,61	170,87
20 000	261,11	243,04	234,78	230,79	228,82	227,83
25 000	326,39	303,80	293,47	288,49	286,02	284,78
30 000	391,66	364,56	352,17	346,19	343,22	341,74
35 000	456,94	425,32	410,86	403,88	400,43	398,69
40 000	522,22	486,08	469,56	461,58	457,63	455,65
45 000	587,49	546,83	528,25	519,28	514,83	512,60
50 000	652,77	607,59	586,94	576,97	572,04	569,56
60 000	783,32	729,11	704,33	692,37	686,44	683,47
70 000	913,88	850,63	821,72	807,76	800,85	797,38
80 000	1044,43	972,15	939,11	923,16	915,26	911,29
90 000	1174,98	1093,66	1056,49	1038,55	1029,66	1025,20
100 000	1305,53	1215,18	1173,88	1153,94	1144,07	1139,11

14¼% Required monthly payment to refund a mortgage loan

terms of loan (in years)

Amount	1	2	3	4	5	10
500	44,86	23,97	17,06	13,63	11,60	7,72
1 000	89,72	47,94	34,11	27,25	23,19	15,44
2 000	179,43	95,88	68,21	54,50	46,38	30,87
3 000	269,15	143,82	102,31	81,75	69,57	46,30
4 000	358,86	191,76	136,41	109,00	92,76	61,74
5 000	448,57	239,70	170,52	136,25	115,94	77,17
6 000	538,29	287,64	204,62	163,50	139,13	92,60
7 000	628,00	335,58	238,72	190,74	162,32	108,04
8 000	717,72	383,52	272,82	217,99	185,51	123,47
9 000	807,43	431,46	306,92	245,34	208,69	138,90
10 000	897,14	479,40	341,03	272,49	231,88	154,34
15 000	1345,71	719,10	511,54	408,73	347,82	231,50
20 000	1794,28	958,79	682,05	544,98	463,76	308,67
25 000	2242,85	1198,49	852,56	681,22	579,70	385,84
30 000	2691,42	1438,19	1023,07	817,46	695,64	463,00
35 000	3139,99	1677,89	1193,58	953,70	811,57	540,17
40 000	3588,56	1917,58	1364,09	1089,95	927,51	617,34
45 000	4037,13	2157,28	1534,60	1226,19	1043,45	694,50
50 000	4485,70	2396,98	1705,11	1362,43	1159,39	771,67
60 000	5382,84	2876,37	2046,13	1634,92	1391,27	926,00
70 000	6279,98	3355,77	2387,16	1907,40	1623,14	1080,33
80 000	7177,12	3835,16	2728,18	2179,89	1855,02	1234,67
90 000	8074,26	4314,56	3069,20	2452,37	2086,90	1389,00
100 000	8971,40	4793,95	3410,22	2724,86	2318,78	1543,33

Amount	terms of loan (in years)					
	15	20	25	30	35	40
500	6,61	6,17	5,96	5,87	5,82	5,80
1 000	13,22	12,33	11,92	11,73	11,64	11,59
2 000	26,43	24,65	23,84	23,46	23,27	23,17
3 000	39,64	36,97	35,76	35,18	34,90	34,76
4 000	52,86	49,29	47,68	46,91	46,53	46,34
5 000	66,07	61,62	59,60	58,63	58,16	57,93
6 000	79,28	73,94	71,52	70,36	69,79	69,51
7 000	92,50	86,26	83,44	82,09	81,42	81,09
8 000	105,71	98,58	95,35	93,81	93,05	92,68
9 000	118,92	110,91	107,27	105,54	104,68	104,26
10 000	132,14	123,23	119,19	117,26	116,32	115,85
15 000	198,20	184,84	178,79	175,89	174,47	173,77
20 000	264,27	246,45	238,38	234,52	232,63	231,69
25 000	330,33	308,07	297,97	293,15	290,78	289,61
30 000	396,40	369,68	357,57	351,78	348,94	347,53
35 000	462,46	431,29	417,16	410,41	407,09	405,45
40 000	528,53	492,90	476,75	469,03	465,25	463,37
45 000	594,59	554,51	536,35	527,66	523,40	521,29
50 000	660,66	616,13	595,94	586,29	581,56	579,21
60 000	792,19	739,35	715,13	703,55	697,87	695,05
70 000	924,92	862,57	834,32	820,81	814,18	810,89
80 000	1057,05	985,80	953,50	938,06	930,49	926,74
90 000	1189,18	1109,02	1072,69	1055,32	1046,80	1042,58
100 000	1321,31	1232,25	1191,88	1172,58	1163,12	1158,42

Amount	terms of loan (in years)					
	1	2	3	4	5	10
500	44,92	24,03	17,11	13,69	11,66	7,79
1 000	89,83	48,06	34,22	27,37	23,31	15,58
2 000	179,65	96,11	68,44	54,74	46,62	31,16
3 000	269,48	144,16	102,66	82,11	69,93	46,73
4 000	359,30	192,21	136,87	109,47	93,24	62,31
5 000	449,13	240,26	171,09	136,84	116,55	77,88
6 000	538,95	288,31	205,31	164,21	139,86	93,46
7 000	628,78	336,36	239,52	191,57	163,17	109,03
8 000	718,60	384,41	273,74	218,94	186,48	124,61
9 000	808,43	432,46	307,96	246,31	209,79	140,18
10 000	898,25	480,51	342,17	273,67	233,10	155,76
15 000	1347,38	720,77	513,26	410,51	349,65	233,63
20 000	1796,50	961,02	684,34	547,34	466,20	311,51
25 000	2245,63	1201,28	855,42	684,18	582,75	389,38
30 000	2694,75	1441,53	1026,51	821,01	699,30	467,26
35 000	3143,88	1681,79	1197,59	957,84	815,85	545,13
40 000	3593,00	1922,04	1368,67	1094,68	932,40	623,01
45 000	4042,13	2162,30	1539,76	1231,51	1048,51	700,88
50 000	4491,25	2402,55	1710,84	1368,35	1165,50	778,76
60 000	5389,50	2883,06	2053,01	1642,02	1398,60	934,51
70 000	6287,75	3363,57	2395,17	1915,68	1631,70	1090,26
80 000	7186,00	3844,08	2737,34	2189,35	1864,80	1246,01
90 000	8084,25	4324,59	3079,51	2463,02	2097,90	1401,76
100 000	8982,50	4805,09	3421,68	2736,69	2331,00	1557,51

Required monthly payment to refund a mortgage loan $14\frac{1}{2}\%$

Amount	terms of loan (in years)					
	15	20	25	30	35	40
500	6,69	6,25	6,05	5,96	5,92	5,89
1 000	13,38	12,50	12,10	11,92	11,83	11,78
2 000	26,75	24,99	24,20	23,83	23,65	23,56
3 000	40,12	37,49	36,30	35,74	35,47	35,34
4 000	53,49	49,98	48,40	47,65	47,29	47,11
5 000	66,86	62,47	60,50	59,57	59,11	58,89
6 000	80,23	74,97	72,60	71,48	70,94	70,67
7 000	93,61	87,46	84,70	83,39	82,76	82,45
8 000	106,98	99,95	96,80	95,30	94,58	94,22
9 000	120,35	112,45	108,90	107,22	106,40	106,00
10 000	133,72	124,94	121,00	119,13	118,22	117,78
15 000	200,58	187,41	181,49	178,69	177,33	176,66
20 000	267,44	249,88	241,99	238,25	236,44	235,55
25 000	334,29	312,35	302,49	297,82	295,55	294,44
30 000	401,15	374,82	362,98	357,38	354,66	353,32
35 000	468,01	437,28	423,48	416,94	413,77	412,21
40 000	534,87	499,75	483,97	476,50	472,88	471,10
45 000	601,72	562,22	544,47	536,06	531,99	529,98
50 000	668,58	624,69	604,97	595,63	591,09	588,87
60 000	802,30	749,63	725,96	714,75	709,31	706,64
70 000	936,01	874,56	846,95	833,87	827,53	824,41
80 000	1069,73	999,50	967,94	953,00	945,75	942,19
90 000	1203,44	1124,44	1088,93	1072,12	1063,97	1059,96
100 000	1337,16	1249,37	1209,93	1191,25	1182,18	1177,73

Amount	terms of loan (in years)					
	1	2	3	4	5	10
500	44,97	24,09	17,17	13,75	11,72	7,86
1 000	89,94	48,17	34,34	27,49	23,44	15,72
2 000	179,88	96,33	68,67	54,98	46,87	31,44
3 000	269,81	144,49	103,00	82,46	70,30	47,16
4 000	359,75	192,65	137,33	109,95	93,73	62,87
5 000	449,68	240,82	171,66	137,43	117,17	78,59
6 000	539,62	288,98	205,99	164,92	140,60	94,31
7 000	629,56	337,14	240,32	192,40	164,03	110,03
8 000	719,49	385,30	274,66	219,89	187,46	125,74
9 000	809,43	433,47	308,99	247,37	210,90	141,46
10 000	899,36	481,63	343,32	274,86	234,33	157,18
15 000	1349,04	722,44	514,98	412,29	351,49	235,76
20 000	1798,72	963,25	686,63	549,71	468,65	314,35
25 000	2248,40	1204,06	858,29	687,14	585,82	392,94
30 000	2698,08	1444,88	1029,95	824,57	702,98	471,52
35 000	3147,76	1685,69	1201,60	961,99	820,14	550,11
40 000	3597,44	1926,50	1373,26	1099,42	937,30	628,70
45 000	4047,12	2167,31	1544,92	1236,85	1054,47	707,28
50 000	4496,80	2408,12	1716,57	1374,27	1171,63	785,87
60 000	5396,16	2889,75	2059,89	1649,13	1405,95	943,04
70 000	6295,52	3371,37	2403,20	1923,98	1640,28	1100,22
80 000	7194,88	3853,00	2746,52	2198,83	1874,60	1257,39
90 000	8094,24	4334,62	3089,83	2473,69	2108,93	1414,56
100 000	8993,60	4816,24	3433,14	2748,54	2343,25	1571,74

Required monthly payment to refund a mortgage loan

14¾%

terms of loan (in years)

Amount	15	20	25	30	35	40
500	6,77	6,34	6,15	6,05	6,01	5,99
1 000	13,54	12,67	12,29	12,10	12,02	11,98
2 000	27,07	25,34	24,57	24,20	24,03	23,95
3 000	40,60	38,00	36,85	36,30	36,04	35,92
4 000	54,13	50,67	49,13	48,40	48,06	47,89
5 000	67,66	63,33	61,41	60,50	60,07	59,86
6 000	81,19	76,00	73,69	72,60	72,08	71,83
7 000	94,72	88,66	85,97	84,70	84,09	83,80
8 000	108,25	101,33	98,25	96,80	96,11	95,77
9 000	121,78	113,99	110,53	108,90	108,12	107,74
10 000	135,31	126,66	122,81	121,00	120,13	119,71
15 000	202,96	189,99	184,21	181,50	180,19	179,56
20 000	270,61	253,31	245,61	241,99	240,26	239,41
25 000	338,27	316,64	307,01	302,49	300,32	299,27
30 000	405,92	379,97	368,41	362,99	360,38	359,12
35 000	473,57	443,30	429,81	423,48	420,45	418,97
40 000	541,22	506,62	491,21	483,98	480,51	478,82
45 000	608,88	569,95	552,61	544,48	540,57	538,68
50 000	676,53	633,28	614,01	604,98	600,64	598,53
60 000	811,83	759,93	736,81	725,97	720,76	718,23
70 000	947,14	886,59	859,61	846,96	840,89	837,94
80 000	1082,44	1013,24	982,41	967,96	961,02	957,64
90 000	1217,75	1139,90	1105,22	1088,95	1081,14	1077,35
100 000	1353,05	1266,55	1228 02	1209,95	1201,27	1197,05

83

Required monthly payment to refund a mortgage loan

terms of loan (in years)

Amount	1	2	3	4	5	10
500	45,03	24,14	17,23	13,81	11,78	7,94
1 000	90,05	48,28	34,45	27,61	23,56	15,87
2 000	180,10	96,55	68,90	55,21	47,12	31,73
3 000	270,15	144,83	103,34	82,82	70,67	47,59
4 000	360,19	193,10	137,79	110,42	94,23	63,45
5 000	450,24	241,37	172,24	138,03	117,78	79,31
6 000	540,29	289,65	206,68	165,63	141,34	95,17
7 000	630,33	337,92	241,13	193,23	164,89	111,03
8 000	720,38	386,20	275,57	220,84	188,45	126,89
9 000	810,43	434,47	310,02	248,44	212,00	142,75
10 000	900,47	482,74	344,47	276,05	235,56	158,61
15 000	1350,71	724,11	516,70	414,07	353,33	237,91
20 000	1800,94	965,48	688,93	552,09	471,11	317,21
25 000	2251,18	1206,85	861,16	690,11	588,89	396,51
30 000	2701,41	1448,22	1033,39	828,13	706,66	475,81
35 000	3151,65	1689,59	1205,62	966,15	824,44	555,11
40 000	3601,88	1930,96	1377,85	1104,17	942,21	634,41
45 000	4052,11	2172,33	1550,08	1242,19	1059,99	713,71
50 000	4502,35	2413,70	1722,31	1380,21	1177,77	793,01
60 000	5402,82	2896,44	2066,78	1656,25	1413,32	951,61
70 000	6303,29	3379,18	2411,24	1932,29	1648,87	1110,21
80 000	7203,76	3861,92	2755,70	2208,33	1884,42	1268,81
90 000	8104,22	4344,66	3100,16	2484,37	2119,98	1427,41
100 000	9004,69	4827,40	3444,62	2760,41	2355,53	1586,01

Required monthly payment to refund a mortgage loan

15%

Amount	terms of loan (in years)					
	15	20	25	30	35	40
500	6,85	6,42	6,24	6,15	6,11	6,09
1 000	13,70	12,84	12,47	12,29	12,21	12,17
2 000	27,39	25,68	24,93	24,58	24,41	24,33
3 000	41,08	38,52	37,39	36,87	36,62	36,50
4 000	54,77	51,36	49,85	49,15	48,82	48,66
5 000	68,46	64,19	62,31	61,44	61,02	60,82
6 000	82,15	77,03	74,77	73,73	73,23	72,99
7 000	95,84	89,87	87,24	86,01	85,43	85,15
8 000	109,53	102,71	99,70	98,30	97,63	97,31
9 000	123,22	115,55	112,16	110,59	109,84	109,48
10 000	136,91	128,38	124,62	122,87	122,04	121,64
15 000	205,36	192,57	186,93	184,31	183,06	182,46
20 000	273,81	256,76	249,23	245,74	244,08	243,28
25 000	342,26	320,95	311,54	307,17	305,10	304,10
30 000	410,71	385,14	373,85	368,61	366,11	364,92
35 000	479,16	449,33	436,16	430,04	427,13	425,74
40 000	547,61	513,52	498,46	491,47	488,15	486,55
45 000	616,06	577,71	560,77	552,91	549,17	547,37
50 000	684,51	641,90	623,08	614,34	610,19	608,19
60 000	821,41	770,28	747,69	737,21	732,22	729,83
70 000	958,31	898,65	872,31	860,07	854,26	851,47
80 000	1095,21	1027,03	996,92	982,94	976,30	973,10
90 000	1232,11	1155,41	1121,54	1105,81	1098,33	1094,74
100 000	1369,01	1283,79	1246,15	1228,67	1220,37	1216,38

terms of loan (in years)

Amount	1	2	3	4	5	10
500	45,08	24,20	17,29	13,87	11,84	8,01
1 000	90,16	48,39	34,57	27,73	23,68	16,01
2 000	180,32	96,78	69,13	55,45	47,36	32,01
3 000	270,48	145,16	103,69	83,17	71,04	48,01
4 000	360,64	193,55	138,25	110,90	94,72	64,02
5 000	450,79	241,93	172,81	138,62	118,40	80,02
6 000	540,95	290,32	207,37	166,34	142,07	96,02
7 000	631,11	338,70	241,93	194,06	165,75	112,03
8 000	721,27	387,09	276,49	221,79	189,43	128,03
9 000	811,43	435,47	311,05	249,51	213,01	144,03
10 000	901,58	483,86	345,62	277,23	236,79	160,04
15 000	1352,37	725,79	518,42	415,85	355,18	240,05
20 000	1803,16	967,71	691,23	554,46	473,57	320,07
25 000	2253,95	1209,64	864,03	693,08	591,96	400,09
30 000	2704,74	1451,57	1036,84	831,69	710,35	480,10
35 000	3155,53	1693,50	1209,64	970,30	828,74	560,12
40 000	3606,32	1935,42	1382,45	1108,92	947,13	640,14
45 000	4057,11	2177,35	1555,25	1247,53	1065,53	720,15
50 000	4507,89	2419,28	1728,06	1386,15	1183,92	800,17
60 000	5409,47	2903,13	2073,67	1663,38	1420,70	960,20
70 000	6311,05	3386,99	2419,28	1940,60	1657,48	1120,23
80 000	7212,63	3870,84	2764,89	2217,83	1894,26	1280,27
90 000	8114,21	4354,70	3110,50	2495,06	2131,05	1440,30
100 000	9015,78	4838,55	3456,11	2772,29	2367,83	1600,33

Amount	terms of loan (in years)					
	15	20	25	30	35	40
500	6,93	6,51	6,33	6,24	6,20	6,18
1 000	13,86	13,02	12,65	12,48	12,40	12,36
2 000	27,71	26.03	25,29	24,95	24,79	24,72
3 000	41,56	39,04	37,93	37,43	37,19	37,08
4 000	55,41	52,05	50,58	49,90	49,58	49,43
5 000	69,26	65,06	63,22	62,38	61,98	61,79
6 000	83,11	78,07	75,86	74,85	74,37	74,15
7 000	96,96	91,08	88,51	87,32	86,77	86,50
8 000	110,81	104,09	101,15	99,80	99,16	98,86
9 000	124,66	117.10	113,79	112,27	111,56	111,22
10 000	138,51	130,11	126,44	124,75	123,95	123,58
15 000	207,76	195,17	189,65	187,12	185,93	185,36
20 000	277,01	260,22	252,87	249,49	247,90	247,15
25 000	346,26	325,27	316,09	311,86	309,87	308,93
30 000	415,51	390,33	379,30	374,23	371,85	370.72
35 000	484,76	455,38	442,52	436,60	433,82	432,50
40 000	554,01	520,43	505,73	498,97	495,80	494,29
45 000	623,26	585,49	568,95	561,34	557,77	556,07
50 000	692,52	650,54	632,17	623,72	61ɔ,74	617,86
60 000	831,02	780,65	758,60	748,46	743,69	741,43
70 000	969,52	910,76	885,03	873,20	867,64	865,00
80 000	1108,02	1040,86	1011,46	997,94	991,59	988,57
90 000	1246,52	1170,97	1137,89	1122,68	1115,53	1112,14
100 000	1385,03	1301,08	1264,33	1247,43	1239,48	1235,71

15½% Required monthly payment to refund a mortgage loan

terms of loan (in years)

Amount	1	2	3	4	5	10
500	45,14	24,25	17,34	13,93	11,91	8,08
1 000	90,27	48,50	34,68	27,85	23,81	16,15
2 000	180,54	97,00	69,36	55,69	47,61	32,30
3 000	270,81	145,50	104,03	83,53	71,41	48,45
4 000	361,08	193,99	138,71	111,37	95,21	64,59
5 000	451,35	242,49	173,39	139,21	119,01	80,74
6 000	541,62	290,99	208,06	167,06	142,81	96,89
7 000	631,89	339,48	242,74	194,90	166,62	113,03
8 000	722,15	387,98	277,41	222,74	190,42	129,18
9 000	812,42	436,48	312,09	250,58	214,22	145,33
10 000	902,69	484,98	346,77	278,42	238,02	161,47
15 000	1354,04	727,46	520,15	417,63	357,03	242,21
20 000	1805,38	969,95	693,53	556,84	476,03	322,94
25 000	2256,72	1212,43	866,91	696,05	595,04	403,68
30 000	2708,07	1454,92	1040,29	835,26	714,05	484,41
35 000	3159,41	1697,40	1213,67	974,47	833,06	565,15
40 000	3610,75	1939,89	1387,05	1113,68	952,06	645,88
45 000	4062,10	2182,37	1560,43	1252,89	1071,07	726,62
50 000	4513,44	2424,86	1733,81	1392,10	1190,08	807,35
60 000	5416,13	2909,83	2080,57	1670,52	1428,09	968,82
70 000	6318,81	3394,80	2427,33	1948,94	1666,11	1130,29
80 000	7221,50	3879,77	2774,09	2227,36	1904,12	1291,76
90 000	8124,19	4364,74	3120,85	2505,77	2142,14	1453,23
100 000	9026,87	4849,71	3467,61	2784,19	2380,15	1614,70

Required monthly payment to refund a mortgage loan 15½%

Amount	terms of loan (in years)					
	15	20	25	30	35	40
500	7,01	6,60	6,42	6,34	6,30	6,28
1 000	14,02	13,19	12,83	12,67	12,59	12,56
2 000	28,03	26,37	25,66	25,33	25,18	25,11
3 000	42,04	39,56	38,48	37,99	37,76	37,66
4 000	56,05	52,74	51,31	50,65	50,35	50,21
5 000	70,06	65,93	64,13	63,31	62,94	62,76
6 000	84,07	79,11	76,96	75,98	75,52	75,31
7 000	98,08	92,29	89,78	88,64	88,11	87,86
8 000	112,09	105,48	102,61	101,30	100,69	100,41
9 000	126,10	118,66	115,43	113,96	113,28	112,96
10 000	140,11	131,85	128,26	126,62	125,87	125,51
15 000	210,17	197,77	192,39	189,93	188,80	188,26
20 000	280,22	263,69	256,51	253,24	251,73	251,01
25 000	350,28	329,61	320,64	316,55	314,66	313,76
30 000	420,33	395,53	384,77	379,86	377,59	376,51
35 000	490,39	461,45	448,89	443,17	440,52	439,27
40 000	560,44	527,37	513,02	506,48	503,45	502,02
45 000	630,50	593,29	577,15	569,79	566,38	564,77
50 000	700,55	659,21	641,27	633,10	629,31	627,52
60 000	840,66	791,05	769,53	759,72	755,17	753,02
70 000	980,77	922,89	897,78	886,34	881,03	878,53
80 000	1120,88	1054,73	1026,03	1012,96	1006,89	1004,03
90 000	1260,99	1186,58	1154,29	1139,59	1132,75	1129,53
100 000	1401,10	1318,42	1282,54	1266,20	1258,61	1255,04

Amount	terms of loan (in years)					
	1	2	3	4	5	10
500	45,19	24,31	17,40	13,99	11,97	8,15
1 000	90,38	48,61	34,80	27,97	23,93	16,30
2 000	180,76	97,22	69,59	55,93	47,85	32,59
3 000	271,14	145,83	104,38	83,89	71,78	48,88
4 000	361,52	194,44	139,17	111,85	95,70	65,17
5 000	451,90	243,05	173,96	139,81	119,63	81,46
6 000	542,28	291,66	208,75	167,77	143,55	97,75
7 000	632,66	340,27	243,54	195,73	167,48	114,04
8 000	723,04	388,87	278,33	223,69	191,40	130,33
9 000	813,42	437,48	313,13	251,65	215,33	146,62
10 000	903,80	486,09	347,92	279,62	239,25	162,92
15 000	1355,70	729,14	521,87	419,42	358,88	244,37
20 000	1807,60	972,18	695,83	559,23	478,50	325,83
25 000	2259,49	1215,22	869,78	699,03	598,13	407,28
30 000	2711,39	1458,27	1043,74	838,84	717,75	488,74
35 000	3163,29	1701,31	1217,70	978,64	837,38	570,19
40 000	3615,19	1944,35	1391,65	1118,45	957,00	651,65
45 000	4067,08	2187,40	1565,61	1258,25	1076,63	733,10
50 000	4518,98	2430,44	1739,56	1398,06	1196,25	814,56
60 000	5422,78	2916,53	2087,48	1677,67	1435,50	977,47
70 000	6326,57	3402,62	2435,39	1957,28	1674,75	1140,38
80 000	7230,37	3888,70	2783,30	2236,89	1914,00	1303,29
90 000	8134,16	4374,79	3131,21	2516,50	2153,25	1466,20
100 000	9037,96	4860,88	3479,12	2796,11	2392,50	1629,11

Required monthly payment to refund a mortgage loan 15¾%

Amount	15	20	25	30	35	40
500	7,09	6,68	6,51	6,43	6,39	6,38
1 000	14,18	13,36	13,01	12,86	12,78	12,75
2 000	28,35	26,72	26,02	25,71	25,56	25,49
3 000	42,52	40,08	39,03	38,56	38,34	38,24
4 000	56,69	53,44	52,04	51,41	51,11	50,98
5 000	70,87	66,80	65,04	64,26	63,89	63,72
6 000	85,04	80,15	78,05	77,11	76,67	76,47
7 000	99,21	93,51	91,06	89,96	89,45	89,21
8 000	113,38	106,87	104,07	102,81	102,22	101,95
9 000	127,55	120,23	117,08	115,66	115,00	114,70
10 000	141,73	133,59	130,08	128,51	127,78	127,44
15 000	212,59	200,38	195,12	192,76	191,67	191,16
20 000	283,45	267,17	260,16	257,01	255,55	254,88
25 000	354,31	333,96	325,20	321,26	319,44	318,59
30 000	425,17	400,75	390,24	385,51	383,33	382,31
35 000	496,03	467,54	455,28	449,76	447,21	446,03
40 000	566,89	534,33	520,32	514,01	511,10	509,75
45 000	637,75	601,12	585,36	578,26	574,99	573,47
50 000	708,61	667,91	650,40	642,51	638,87	637,18
60 000	850,33	801,49	780,48	771,01	766,65	764,62
70 000	992,06	935,07	910,55	899,51	894,42	892,06
80 000	1133,78	1068,65	1040,63	1028,01	1022,19	1019,49
90 000	1275,50	1202,23	1170,71	1156,51	1149,97	1146,93
100 000	1417,22	1335,81	1300,79	1285,01	1277,74	1274,36

terms of loan (in years)

Required monthly payment to refund a mortgage loan

terms of loan (in years)

Amount	1	2	3	4	5	10
500	45,25	24,37	17,46,	14,05	12,03	8,22
1 000	90,50	48,73	34,91	28,09	24,05	16,44
2 000	180,99	97,45	69,82	56,17	48,10	32,88
3 000	271,48	146,17	104,72	84,25	72,15	49,31
4 000	361,97	194,89	139,63	112,33	96,20	65,75
5 000	452,46	243,61	174,54	140,41	120,25	82,18
6 000	542,95	292,33	209,44	168,49	144,30	98,62
7 000	633,44	341,05	244,35	196,57	168,35	115,05
8 000	723,93	389,77	279,26	224,65	192,39	131,49
9 000	814,42	438,49	314,16	252,73	216,44	147,93
10 000	904,91	487,21	349,07	280,81	240,49	164,36
15 000	1357,36	730,81	523,60	421,21	360,73	246,54
20 000	1809,81	974,41	698,13	561,61	480,98	328,72
25 000	2262,26	1218,02	872,67	702,02	601,22	410,90
30 000	2714,71	1461,62	1047,20	842,42	721,46	493,08
35 000	3167,17	1705,22	1221,73	982,82	841,71	575,25
40 000	3619,62	1948,82	1396,26	1123,22	961,95	657,43
45 000	4072,07	2192,42	1570,79	1263,63	1082,19	739,61
50 000	4524,52	2436,03	1745,33	1404,03	1202,44	821,79
60 000	5429,42	2923,23	2094,39	1684,83	1442,92	986,15
70 000	6334,33	3410,43	2443,45	1965,64	1683,41	1150,50
80 000	7239,23	3897,64	2792,52	2246,44	1923,89	1314,86
90 000	8144,13	4384,84	3141,58	2527,25	2164,38	1479,22
100 000	9049,04	4872,05	3490,65	2808,05	2404,87	1643,58

Required monthly payment to refund a mortgage loan   16%

terms of loan (in years)

Amount	15	20	25	30	35	40
500	7,17	6,77	6,60	6,52	6,49	6,47
1 000	14,34	13,54	13,20	13,04	12,97	12,94
2 000	28,67	27,07	26,39	26,08	25,94	25,88
3 000	43,01	40,60	39,58	39,12	38,91	38,82
4 000	57,34	54,13	52,77	52,16	51,88	51,75
5 000	71,67	67,67	65,96	65,20	64,85	64,69
6 000	86,01	81,20	79,15	78,23	77,82	77,63
7 000	100,34	94,73	92,34	91,27	90,79	90,56
8 000	114,68	108,26	105,53	104,31	103,76	103,50
9 000	129,01	121,80	118,72	117,35	116,72	116,44
10 000	143,34	135,33	131,91	130,39	129,69	129,37
15 000	215,01	202,99	197,87	195,58	194,54	194,06
20 000	286,68	270,65	263,82	260,77	259,38	258,74
25 000	358,35	338,31	329,77	325,96	324,22	323,43
30 000	430,02	405,98	395,73	391,15	389,07	388,11
35 000	501,69	473,64	461,68	456,34	453,91	452,80
40 000	573,36	541,30	527,63	521,53	518,76	517,48
45 000	645,03	608,96	593,59	586,72	583,60	582,16
50 000	716,70	676,62	659,54	651,92	648,44	646,85
60 000	860,04	811,95	791,45	782,30	778,13	776,22
70 000	1003,38	947,27	923,35	912,68	907,82	905,59
80 000	1146,72	1082,59	1055,26	1043,06	1037,51	1034,95
90 000	1290,06	1217,92	1187,17	1173,44	1167,20	1164,32
100 000	1433,40	1353,24	1319,07	1303,83	1296,88	1293,69

16¼% Required monthly payment to refund a mortgage loan

Amount	\multicolumn{6}{c}{terms of loan (in years)}
	1	2	3	4	5	10
500	45,31	24,42	17,52	14,10	12,09	8,30
1 000	90,61	48,84	35,03	28,20	24,18	16,59
2 000	181,21	97,67	70,05	56,40	48,35	33,17
3 000	271,81	146,50	105,07	84,60	72,52	49,75
4 000	362,41	195,33	140,09	112,80	96,70	66,33
5 000	453,01	244,17	175,11	141,00	120,87	82,91
6 000	543,61	293,00	210,14	169,20	145,04	99,49
7 000	634,21	341,83	245,16	197,40	169,21	116,07
8 000	724,81	390,66	280,18	225,60	193,39	132,65
9 000	815,41	439,49	315,20	253,80	217,56	149,23
10 000	906,02	488,33	350,22	282,00	241,73	165,81
15 000	1359,02	732,49	525,33	423,00	362,59	248,72
20 000	1812,03	976,65	700,44	564,00	483,46	331,62
25 000	2265,03	1220,81	875,55	705,00	604,32	414,52
30 000	2718,04	1464,97	1050,66	846,00	725,18	497,43
35 000	3171,04	1709,13	1225,77	987,00	846,04	580,33
40 000	3624,05	1953,29	1400,87	1128,00	966,91	663,24
45 000	4077,05	2197,45	1575,98	1269,00	1087,77	746,14
50 000	4530,06	2441,61	1751,09	1410,00	1208,63	829,04
60 000	5436,07	2929,93	2101,31	1692,00	1450,36	994,85
70 000	6342,08	3418,25	2451,53	1974,00	1692,08	1160,66
80 000	7248,09	3906,58	2801,74	2256,00	1933,81	1326,47
90 000	8154,10	4394,90	3151,96	2538,00	2175,53	1492,27
100 000	9060,11	4883,22	3502,18	2820,00	2417,26	1658,08

Required monthly payment to refund a mortgage loan 16¼%

Amount	terms of loan (in years)					
	15	20	25	30	35	40
500	7,25	6,86	6,69	6,62	6,59	6,57
1 000	14,50	13,71	13,38	13,23	13,17	13,14
2 000	29,00	27,42	26,75	26,46	26,33	26,27
3 000	43,49	41,13	40,13	39,68	39,49	39,40
4 000	57,99	54,83	53,50	52,91	52,65	52,53
5 000	72,49	68,54	66,87	66,14	65,81	65,66
6 000	86,98	82,25	80,25	79,36	78,97	78,79
7 000	101,48	95,96	93,62	92,59	92,13	91,92
8 000	115,97	109,66	107,00	105,82	105,29	105,05
9 000	130,47	123,37	120,37	119,04	118,45	118,18
10 000	144,97	137,08	133,74	132,27	131,61	131,31
15 000	217,45	205,61	200,61	198,40	197,41	196,96
20 000	289,93	274,15	267,48	264,54	263,21	262,61
25 000	362,41	342,68	334,35	330,67	329,01	328,26
30 000	434,89	411,22	401,22	396,80	394,81	393,91
35 000	507,37	479,76	468,09	462,94	460,61	459,56
40 000	579,85	548,29	534,96	529,07	526,41	525,21
45 000	652,33	616,83	601,83	595,20	592,22	590,86
50 000	724,81	685,36	668,70	661,93	658,02	656,51
60 000	869,78	822,43	802,44	793,60	789,62	787,81
70 000	1014,74	959,51	936,17	925,87	921,22	919,11
80 000	1159,70	1096,58	1069,91	1058,13	1052,82	1050,41
90 000	1304,66	1233,65	1203,65	1190,40	1184,43	1181,71
100 000	1449,62	1370,72	1337,39	1322,66	1316,03	1313,01

Required monthly payment to refund a mortgage loan

Amount	terms of loan (in years)					
	1	2	3	4	5	10
500	45,36	24,48	17,57	14,16	12,15	8,37
1 000	90,72	48,95	35,14	28,32	24,30	16,73
2 000	181,43	97,89	70,28	56,64	48,60	33,46
3 000	272,14	146,84	105,42	84,96	72,90	50,18
4 000	362,85	195,78	140,55	113,28	97,19	66,91
5 000	453,56	244,72	175,69	141,60	121,49	83,64
6 000	544,28	293,67	210,83	169,92	145,79	100,36
7 000	634,99	342,61	245,97	198,24	170,08	117,09
8 000	725,70	391,56	281,10	226,56	194,38	133,82
9 000	816,41	440,50	316,24	254,88	218,68	150,54
10 000	907,12	489,44	351,38	283,20	242,97	167,27
15 000	1360,68	734,16	527,06	424,80	364,46	250,90
20 000	1814,24	978,88	702,75	566,40	485,94	334,53
25 000	2267,80	1223,60	878,44	708,00	607,42	418,16
30 000	2721,36	1468,32	1054,12	849,60	728,91	501,79
35 000	3174,92	1713,04	1229,81	991,20	850,39	585,43
40 000	3628,48	1957,76	1405,49	1132,79	971,87	669,06
45 000	4082,04	2202,48	1581,18	1274,39	1093,36	752,69
50 000	4535,60	2447,20	1756,87	1415,99	1214,84	836,32
60 000	5442,72	2936,64	2108,24	1699,19	1457,81	1003,58
70 000	6349,83	3426,08	2459,61	1982,39	1700,78	1170,85
80 000	7256,95	3915,52	2810,98	2265,58	1943,74	1338,11
90 000	8164,07	4404,96	3162,35	2548,78	2186,71	1505,37
100 000	9071,19	4894,40	3513,73	2831,98	2429,68	1672,63

Amount	\multicolumn{6}{c}{terms of loan (in years)}					
	15	20	25	30	35	40
500	7,33	6,95	6,78	6,71	6,68	6,67
1 000	14,66	13,89	13,56	13,42	13,36	13,33
2 000	29,32	27,77	27,12	26,84	26,71	26,65
3 000	43,98	41,65	40,68	40,25	40,06	39,97
4 000	58,64	55,53	54,23	53,67	53,41	53,30
5 000	73,30	69,42	67,79	67,08	66,76	66,62
6 000	87,96	83,30	81,35	80,50	80,12	79,94
7 000	102,62	97,18	94,91	93,91	93,47	93,27
8 000	117,28	111,06	108,46	107,33	106,82	106,59
9 000	131,94	124,95	122,02	120,74	120,17	119,91
10 000	146,60	138,83	135,58	134,16	133,52	133,24
15 000	219,89	208,24	203,37	201,23	200,28	199,85
20 000	293,19	277,65	271,15	268,31	267,04	266,47
25 000	366,48	347,07	338,94	335,38	333,80	333,09
30 000	439,78	416,48	406,73	402,46	400,56	399,70
35 000	513,07	485,89	474,51	469,54	467,32	466,32
40 000	586,37	555,30	542,30	536,61	534,08	532,94
45 000	659,66	624,71	610,09	603,69	600,84	599,55
50 000	732,96	694,13	677,87	670,76	667,60	666,17
60 000	879,55	832,95	813,45	804,92	801,11	799,40
70 000	1026,14	971,78	949,02	939,07	934,63	932,64
80 000	1172,73	1110,60	1084,59	1073,22	1068,15	1065,87
90 000	1319,32	1249,42	1220,17	1207,37	1201,67	1199,10
100 000	1465,91	1388,25	1355,74	1341,52	1335,19	1332,34

16¾% Required monthly payment to refund a mortgage loan

Amount	terms of loan (in years)					
	1	2	3	4	5	10
500	45,42	24,53	17,63	14,22	12,22	8,44
1 000	90,83	49,06	35,26	28,44	24,43	16,88
2 000	181,65	98,12	70,51	56,88	48,85	33,75
3 000	272,47	147,17	105,76	85,32	73,27	50,62
4 000	363,30	196,23	141,02	113,76	97,69	67,49
5 000	454,12	245,28	176,27	142,20	122,11	84,37
6 000	544,94	294,34	211,52	170,64	146,53	101,24
7 000	635,76	343,40	246,77	199,08	170,95	118,11
8 000	726,59	392,45	282,03	227,52	195,37	134,98
9 000	817,41	441,51	317,28	255,96	219,79	151,86
10 000	908,23	490,56	352,53	284,40	244,22	168,73
15 000	1362,34	735,84	528,80	426,60	366,32	253,09
20 000	1816,46	981,12	705,06	568,80	488,43	337,45
25 000	2270,57	1226,40	881,32	710,99	610,53	421,81
30 000	2724,68	1471,68	1057,59	853,19	732,64	506,17
35 000	3178,79	1716,96	1233,85	995,39	854,74	590,53
40 000	3632,91	1962,23	1410,12	1137,59	976,85	674,89
45 000	4087,02	2207,51	1586,38	1279,79	1098,95	759,26
50 000	4541,13	2452,79	1762,64	1421,98	1221,06	843,62
60 000	5449,36	2943,35	2115,17	1706,38	1465,27	1012,34
70 000	6357,58	3433,91	2467,70	1990,78	1709,48	1181,06
80 000	7265,81	3924,46	2820,23	2275,17	1953,69	1349,78
90 000	8174,04	4415,02	3172,75	2559,57	2197,90	1518,51
100 000	9082,26	4905,58	3525,28	2843,96	2442,12	1687,23

Required monthly payment to refund a mortgage loan   16¾%

Amount	terms of loan (in years)					
	15	20	25	30	35	40
500	7,42	7,03	6,88	6,81	6,78	6,76
1 000	14,83	14,06	13,75	13,61	13,55	13,52
2 000	29,65	28,12	27,49	27,21	27,09	27,04
3 000	44,47	42,18	41,23	40,82	40,64	40,55
4 000	59,29	56,24	54,97	54,42	54,18	54,07
5 000	74,12	70,30	68,71	68,02	67,72	67,59
6 000	88,94	84,35	82,45	81,63	81,27	81,10
7 000	103,76	98,41	96,19	95,23	94,81	94,62
8 000	118,58	112,47	109,93	108,84	108,35	108,14
9 000	133,41	126,53	123,68	122,44	121,90	121,65
10 000	148,23	140,59	137,42	136,04	135,44	135,17
15 000	222,34	210,88	206,12	204,06	203,16	202,75
20 000	296,45	281,17	274,83	272,08	270,87	270,33
25 000	370,56	351,46	343,53	340,10	338,59	337,92
30 000	444,67	421,75	412,24	408,12	406,31	405,50
35 000	518,79	492,04	480,94	476,14	474,02	473,08
40 000	592,90	562,33	549,65	544,16	541,74	540,66
45 000	667,01	632,62	618,36	612,18	609,46	608,25
50 000	741,12	702,91	687,06	680,20	677,17	675,83
60 000	889,34	843,49	824,47	816,24	812,61	810,99
70 000	1037,57	984,07	961,88	952,28	948,04	946,16
80 000	1185,79	1124,65	1099,30	1088,32	1083,48	1081,32
90 000	1334,01	1265,23	1236,71	1224,36	1218,91	1216,49
100 000	1482,23	1405,82	1374,12	1360,39	1354,34	1351,65

Required monthly payment to refund a mortgage loan

Amount	terms of loan (in years)					
	1	2	3	4	5	10
500	45,47	24,59	17,69	14,28	12,28	8,51
1 000	90,94	49,17	35,37	28,56	24,55	17,02
2 000	181,87	98,34	70,74	57,12	49,10	34,04
3 000	272,80	147,51	106,11	85,68	73,64	51,06
4 000	363,74	196.68	141,48	114,24	98,19	68,08
5 000	454,67	245,84	176,85	142,80	122,73	85,10
6 000	545,60	295,01	212,22	171,36	147,28	102,12
7 000	636,54	344,18	247,58	199,92	171,83	119,14
8 000	727,47	397,35	282,95	228,48	196,37	136,15
9 000	818,40	442,51	318,32	257,04	220,92	153,17
10 000	909,34	491,68	353,69	285,60	245,46	170,19
15 000	1364,00	737,52	530,53	428,40	368,19	255,28
20 000	1818,67	983,36	707,37	571,20	490,92	340,38
25 000	2273,34	1229,19	884,22	714,00	613,65	425,47
30 000	2728,00	1475,03	1061,06	856,79	736,38	510,56
35 000	3182,67	1720,87	1237,90	999,59	859,11	595,66
40 000	3637,33	1966,71	1414,74	1142,39	981,83	680,75
45 000	4092,00	2212,55	1591,58	1285,19	1104,56	765,84
50 000	4546,67	2458,38	1768,43	1427,99	1227,29	850,94
60 000	5456,00	2950,06	2122,11	1713,58	1472,75	1021,12
70 000	6365,33	3441,74	2475,79	1999,18	1718,21	1191,31
80 000	7274,66	3933,41	2829,48	2284,78	1963,66	1361,50
90 000	8184,00	4425,09	3183,16	2570,37	2209,12	1531,68
100 000	9093,33	4916,76	3536,85	2855,97	2454,58	1701,87

Required monthly payment to refund a mortgage loan 17%

Amount	terms of loan (in years)					
	15	20	25	30	35	40
500	7,50	7,12	6,97	6,90	6,87	6,86
1 000	14,99	14,24	13,93	13,80	13,74	13,71
2 000	29,98	28,47	27,86	27,59	27,47	27,42
3 000	44,96	42,71	41,78	41,38	41,21	41,13
4 000	59,95	56,94	55,71	55,18	54,94	54,84
5 000	74,94	71,18	69,63	68,97	68,68	68,55
6 000	89,92	85,41	83,56	82,76	82,41	82,26
7 000	104,91	99,64	97,48	96,55	96,15	95,97
8 000	119,89	113,88	111,41	110,35	109,88	109,68
9 000	134,88	128,11	125,33	124,14	123,62	123,39
10 000	149,87	142,35	139,26	137,93	137,35	137,10
15 000	224,80	213,52	208,88	206,90	206,03	205,65
20 000	299,73	284,69	278,51	275,86	274,70	274,20
25 000	374,66	355,86	348,13	344,82	343,38	342,74
30 000	449,59	427,03	417,76	413,79	412,05	411,29
35 000	524,52	498,20	487,39	482,75	480,73	479,84
40 000	599,45	569,37	557,01	551,72	549,40	548,39
45 000	674,38	640,54	626,64	620,68	618,08	616,94
50 000	749,31	711,72	696,26	689,64	686,75	685,48
60 000	899,17	854,06	835,52	827,57	824,10	822,58
70 000	1049,03	996,40	974,77	965,50	961,45	959,68
80 000	1198,89	1138,74	1114,02	1103,43	1098,80	1096,77
90 000	1348,75	1281,08	1253,27	1241,35	1236,15	1233,87
100 000	1498,61	1423,43	1392,52	1379,28	1373,50	1370,96

Amount	terms of loan (in years)					
	1	2	3	4	5	10
500	45,53	24,64	17,75	14,34	12,34	8,59
1 000	91,05	49,28	35,49	28,68	24,68	17,17
2 000	182,09	98,56	70,97	57,36	49,35	34,34
3 000	273,14	147,94	106,46	86,04	74,02	51,50
4 000	364,18	197,12	141,94	114,72	98,69	68,67
5 000	455,22	246,40	177,43	143,40	123,36	85,83
6 000	546,27	295,68	212,91	172,08	148,03	103,00
7 000	637,31	344,96	248,39	200,76	172,70	120,16
8 000	728,36	394,24	283,88	229,44	197,37	137,33
9 000	819,40	443,52	319,36	258,12	222,04	154,49
10 000	910,44	492,80	354,85	286,80	246,71	171,66
15 000	1365,66	739,20	532,27	430,20	370,06	257,49
20 000	1820,88	985,59	709,69	573,60	493,42	343,31
25 000	2276,10	1231,99	887,11	717,00	616,77	429,14
30 000	2731,32	1478,39	1064,53	860,40	740,12	514,97
35 000	3186,54	1724,79	1241,95	1003,80	863,48	600,80
40 000	3641,76	1971,18	1419,37	1147,20	986,83	686,62
45 000	4096,98	2217,58	1596,79	1290,60	1110,18	772,45
50 000	4552,20	2463,98	1774,21	1434,00	1233,53	858,28
60 000	5462,64	2956,77	2129,06	1720,80	1480,24	1029,93
70 000	6373,08	3449,57	2483,90	2007,60	1726,95	1201,59
80 000	7283,52	3942,36	2838,74	2294,40	1973,65	1373,24
90 000	8193,95	4435,16	3193,58	2581,19	2220,36	1544,90
100 000	9104,39	4927,95	3548,42	2867,99	2467,06	1716,55

	terms of loan (in years)					
Amount	15	20	25	30	35	40
500	7,58	7,21	7,06	7,00	6,97	6,96
1 000	15,16	14,42	14,11	13,99	13,93	13,91
2 000	30,31	28,83	28,22	27,97	27,86	27,81
3 000	45,46	43,24	42,33	41,95	41,78	41,71
4 000	60,61	57,65	56,44	55,93	55,71	55,62
5 000	75,76	72,06	70,55	69,91	69,64	69,52
6 000	90,91	86,47	84,66	83,90	83,56	83,42
7 000	106,06	100,88	98,77	97,88	97,49	97,32
8 000	121,21	115,29	112,88	111,86	111,42	111,23
9 000	136,36	129,70	126,99	125,84	125,34	125,13
10 000	151,51	144,11	141,10	139,82	139,27	139,03
15 000	227,26	216,16	211,65	209,73	208,90	208,54
20 000	303,01	288,22	282,19	279,64	278,54	278,06
25 000	378,76	360,27	352,74	349,55	348,17	347,57
30 000	454,51	432,32	423,29	419,46	417,80	417,08
35 000	530,27	504,38	493,84	489,37	487,44	486,60
40 000	606,02	576,43	564,38	559,27	557,07	556,11
45 000	681,77	648,48	634,93	629,18	626,70	625,62
50 000	757,52	720,54	705,48	699,09	696,33	695,14
60 000	909,02	864,64	846,57	838,91	835,60	834,16
70 000	1060,53	1008,75	987,67	978,73	974,87	973,19
80 000	1212,03	1152,86	1128,76	1118,54	1114,13	1112,21
90 000	1363,53	1296,96	1269,86	1258,36	1253,40	1251,24
100 000	1515,04	1441,07	1410,95	1398,18	1392,66	1390,27

17½% Required monthly payment to refund a mortgage loan

terms of loan (in years)

Amount	1	2	3	4	5	10
500	45,58	24,70	17,81	14,41	12,40	8,66
1 000	91,16	49,40	35,61	28,81	24,80	17,32
2 000	182,31	98,79	71,21	57,61	49,60	34,63
3 000	273,47	148,18	106,81	86,41	74,39	51,94
4 000	364,62	197,57	142,41	115,21	99,19	69,26
5 000	455,78	246,96	178,01	144,01	123,98	86,57
6 000	546,93	296,35	213,61	172,81	148,78	103,88
7 000	638,09	345,74	249,21	201,61	173,57	121,19
8 000	729,24	395,14	284,81	230,41	198,37	138,51
9 000	820,40	444,53	320,41	259,21	223,17	155,82
10 000	911,55	493,92	356,01	288,01	247,96	173,13
15 000	1367,32	740,88	534,01	432,01	371,94	259,70
20 000	1823,10	987,83	712,01	576,01	495,92	346,26
25 000	2278,87	1234,79	890,01	720,01	619,90	432,82
30 000	2734,64	1481,75	1068,01	864,01	743,88	519,39
35 000	3190,41	1728,70	1246,01	1008,02	867,85	605,95
40 000	3646,19	1975,66	1424,01	1152,02	991,83	692,51
45 000	4101,96	2222,62	1602,01	1296,02	1115,81	779,08
50 000	4557,73	2469,58	1780,01	1440,02	1239,79	865,64
60 000	5469,28	2963,49	2136,01	1728,02	1487,75	1038,77
70 000	6380,82	3457,40	2492,01	2016,03	1735,70	1211,90
80 000	7292,37	3951,32	2848,01	2304,03	1983,66	1385,02
90 000	8203,91	4445,23	3204,01	2592,03	2231,62	1558,15
100 000	9115,46	4939,15	3560,01	2880,03	2479,57	1731,28

Required monthly payment to refund a mortgage loan   17½%

Amount	terms of loan (in years)					
	15	20	25	30	35	40
500	7,66	7,30	7,15	7,09	7,06	7,05
1 000	15,32	14,59	14,30	14,18	14,12	14,10
2 000	30,64	29,18	28,59	28,35	28,24	28,20
3 000	45,95	43,77	42,89	42,52	42,36	42,29
4 000	61,27	58,36	57,18	56,69	56,48	56,39
5 000	76,58	72,94	71,48	70,86	70,60	70,48
6 000	91,90	87,53	85,77	85,03	84,71	84,58
7 000	107,21	102,12	100,06	99,20	98,83	98,67
8 000	122,53	116,71	114,09	113,37	112,95	112,77
9 000	137,84	131,29	128,65	127,54	127,07	126,87
10 000	153,16	145,88	142,95	141,71	141,19	140,96
15 000	229,73	218,82	214,42	212,57	211,78	211,44
20 000	306,31	291,76	285,89	283,42	282,37	281,92
25 000	382,88	364,69	357,36	354,28	352,96	352,39
30 000	459,46	437,63	428,83	425,13	423,55	422,87
35 000	536,03	510,57	500,30	495,98	494,14	493,35
40 000	612,61	583,51	571,77	566,84	564,73	563,83
45 000	689,18	656,44	643,24	637,69	635,32	634,31
50 000	765,76	729,38	714,71	708,55	705,92	704,78
60 000	918,91	875,26	857,65	850,25	847,10	845,74
70 000	1072,06	1021,13	1000,59	991,96	988,28	986,70
80 000	1225,21	1167,01	1143,53	1133,67	1129,46	1127,65
90 000	1378,36	1312,88	1286,47	1275,38	1270,64	1268,61
100 000	1531,51	1458,76	1429,41	1417,09	1411,83	1409,56

Amount	terms of loan (in years)					
	1	2	3	4	5	10
500	45,64	24,76	17,86	14,47	12,47	8,74
1 000	91,27	49,51	35,72	28,93	24,93	17,47
2 000	182,54	99,01	71,44	57,85	49,85	34,93
3 000	273,80	148,52	107,15	86,77	74,77	52,39
4 000	365,07	198,02	142,87	115,69	99,69	69,85
5 000	456,33	247,52	178,59	144,61	124,61	87,31
6 000	547,60	297,03	214,30	173,53	149,53	104,77
7 000	638,86	346,53	250,02	202,45	174,45	122,23
8 000	730,13	396,03	285,73	231,37	199,37	139,69
9 000	821,39	445,54	321,45	260,29	224,29	157,15
10 000	912,66	495,04	357,17	289,21	249,21	174,61
15 000	1368,98	742,56	535,75	433,82	373,82	261,91
20 000	1825,31	990,07	714,33	578,42	498,42	349,21
25 000	2281,63	1237,59	892,91	723,03	623,03	436,51
30 000	2737,96	1485,11	1071,49	867,63	747,63	523,82
35 000	3194,28	1732,62	1250,07	1012,23	872,24	611,12
40 000	3650,61	1980,14	1428,65	1156,84	996,84	698,42
45 000	4106,93	2227,66	1607,23	1301,44	1121,45	785,72
50 000	4563,26	2475,17	1785,81	1446,05	1246,05	873,02
60 000	5475,91	2970,21	2142,97	1735,26	1495,26	1047,63
70 000	6388,56	3465,24	2500,13	2024,46	1744,47	1222,23
80 000	7301,21	3960,27	2857,29	2313,67	1993,68	1396,84
90 000	8213,86	4455,31	3214,45	2602,88	2242,89	1571,44
100 000	9126,51	4950,34	3571,61	2892,09	2492,10	1746,04

Required monthly payment to refund a mortgage loan $17\frac{3}{4}\%$

Amount	terms of loan (in years)					
	15	20	25	30	35	40
500	7,75	7,39	7,24	7,18	7,16	7,15
1 000	15,49	14,77	14,48	14,36	14,31	14,29
2 000	30,97	29,53	28,96	28,72	28,62	28,58
3 000	46,45	44,30	43,44	43,08	42,93	42,87
4 000	61,93	59,06	57,92	57,44	57,24	57,16
5 000	77,41	73,83	72,40	71,80	71,55	71,45
6 000	92,89	88,59	86,88	86,16	85,86	85,74
7 000	108,37	103,36	101,36	100,52	100,17	100,02
8 000	123,85	118,12	115,84	114,88	114,48	114,31
9 000	139,33	132,89	130,31	129,24	128,79	128,60
10 000	154,81	147,65	144,79	143,60	143,10	142,89
15 000	232,21	221,48	217,19	215,40	214,65	214,33
20 000	309,61	295,30	289,58	287,20	286,20	285,77
25 000	387,01	369,12	361,98	359,00	357,75	357,22
30 000	464,41	442,95	434,37	430,80	429,30	428,66
35 000	541,81	516,77	506,76	502,60	500,85	500,10
40 000	619,21	590,59	579,16	574,40	572,40	571,54
45 000	696,61	664,42	661,55	646,20	643,95	642,99
50 000	774,02	738,24	723,95	718,00	715,50	714,43
60 000	928,82	885,89	868,73	861,60	858,59	857,31
70 000	1083,62	1033,54	1013,52	1005,20	1001,69	1000,20
80 000	1238,42	1181,18	1158,31	1148,80	1144,79	1143,08
90 000	1393,22	1328,83	1303,10	1292,40	1287,89	1285,97
100 000	1548,03	1476,48	1447,89	1436,00	1430,99	1428,85

Required monthly payment to refund a mortgage loan

Amount	terms of loan (in years)					
	1	2	3	4	5	10
500	45,69	24,81	17,92	14,53	12,53	8,81
1 000	91,38	49,62	35,84	29,05	25,05	17,61
2 000	182,76	99,24	71,67	58,09	50,10	35,22
3 000	274,13	148,85	107,50	87,13	75,14	52,83
4 000	365,51	198,47	143,33	116,17	100,19	70,44
5 000	456,88	248,08	179,17	145,21	125,24	88,05
6 000	548,26	297,70	215,00	174,25	150,28	105,66
7 000	639,63	347,31	250,83	203,30	175,33	123,26
8 000	731,01	396,93	286,66	232,34	200,38	140,87
9 000	822,39	446,54	322,49	261,38	225,42	158,48
10 000	913,76	496,16	358,33	290,42	250,47	176,09
15 000	1370,64	744,24	537,49	435,63	375,70	264,13
20 000	1827,52	992,31	716,64	580,84	500,94	352,17
25 000	2284,40	1240,39	895,81	726,04	626,17	440,22
30 000	2741,27	1488,47	1074,97	871,25	751,40	528,26
35 000	3198,15	1736,54	1254,13	1016,46	876,63	616,30
40 000	3655,03	1984,62	1433,29	1161,67	1001,87	704,34
45 000	4111,91	2232,70	1612,45	1306,88	1127,10	792,39
50 000	4568,79	2480,77	1791,61	1452,08	1252,33	880,43
60 000	5482,54	2976,93	2149,93	1742,50	1502,80	1056,51
70 000	6396,30	3473,08	2508,25	2032,92	1753,26	1232,60
80 000	7310,06	3969,23	2866,57	2323,33	2003,73	1408,68
90 000	8223,81	4465,39	3224,89	2613,75	2254,19	1584,77
100 000	9137,57	4961,54	3583,22	2904,16	2504,66	1760,85

Required monthly payment to refund a mortgage loan

18%

Amount	terms of loan (in years)					
	15	20	25	30	35	40
500	7,83	7,48	7,34	7,28	7,26	7,25
1 000	15,65	14,95	14,67	14,55	14,51	14,49
2 000	31,30	29,89	29,33	29,10	29,01	28,97
3 000	46,94	44,83	44,00	43,65	43,51	43,45
4 000	62,59	59,77	58,66	58,20	58,01	57.93
5 000	78,23	74,72	73,32	72,75	72,51	72,41
6 000	93,88	89,66	87,99	87,30	87,01	86,89
7 000	109,53	104,60	102,65	101,85	101,51	101,37
8 000	125,17	119,54	117,32	116,40	116,02	115,86
9 000	140,82	134,49	131,98	130,95	130,52	130,34
10 000	156,46	149,43	146,64	145,50	145,02	144,82
15 000	234,69	224,14	219,96	218,24	217,53	217,22
20 000	312,92	298,85	293,28	290,99	290,03	289,63
25 000	391,15	373,56	366,60	363,74	362,54	362,04
30 000	469,38	448,27	439,92	436,48	435,05	434,44
35 000	547,61	522,99	513,24	509,23	507,55	506,85
40 000	625,84	597,70	586,56	581,97	580,06	579,26
45 000	704,07	672,41	659,88	654,72	652,57	651,66
50 000	782,30	747,12	733,19	727,47	725,07	724,07
60 000	938,76	896,54	879,83	872,96	870,09	868,88
70 000	1095,21	1045,97	1026,47	1018,45	1015,10	1013,69
80 000	1251,67	1195,39	1173,11	1163,94	1160,12	1158,51
90 000	1408,13	1344,81	1319,75	1309,44	1305,13	1303,32
100 000	1564,59	1494,24	1466.38	1454,93	1450,14	1448,13

18¼% Required monthly payment to refund a mortgage loan

Amount	1	2	3	4	5	10
500	45,75	24,87	17,98	14,59	12,59	8,88
1 000	91,49	49,73	35,95	29,17	25,18	17,76
2 000	182,98	99,46	71,90	58,33	50,35	35,52
3 000	274,46	149,19	107,85	87,49	75,52	53,28
4 000	365,95	198,91	143,80	116,65	100,69	71,03
5 000	457,44	248,64	179,75	145,82	125,87	88,79
6 000	548,92	298,37	215,69	174,98	151,04	106,55
7 000	640,41	348,10	251,64	204,14	176,21	124,30
8 000	731,89	397,82	287,59	233,30	201,38	142,06
9 000	823,38	447,55	323,54	262,47	226,56	159,82
10 000	914,87	497,28	359,49	291,63	251,73	177,57
15 000	1372,30	745,92	539,23	437,44	377,59	266,36
20 000	1829,73	994,55	718,97	583,25	503,45	355,14
25 000	2287,16	1243,19	898,71	729,07	629,31	443,93
30 000	2744,59	1491,83	1078,45	874,88	755,17	532,71
35 000	3202,02	1740,46	1258,19	1020,69	881,03	621,50
40 000	3659,45	1989,10	1437,94	1166,50	1006,89	710,28
45 000	4116,88	2237,74	1617,68	1312,32	1132,76	799,07
50 000	4574,31	2486,38	1797,42	1458,13	1258,62	887,85
60 000	5489,17	2983,65	2156,90	1749,75	1510,34	1065,42
70 000	6404,04	3480,92	2516,38	2041,38	1762,02	1242,99
80 000	7318,90	3978,20	2875,87	2333,00	2013,78	1420,56
90 000	8233,76	4475,47	3235,35	2624,63	2265,51	1598,13
100 000	9148,62	4972,75	3594,83	2916,25	2517,23	1775,70

Required monthly payment to refund a mortgage loan — 18¼%

Amount	terms of loan (in years)					
	15	20	25	30	35	40
500	7,91	7,57	7,43	7,37	7,35	7,34
1 000	15,82	15,13	14,85	14,74	14,70	14,68
2 000	31,63	30,25	29,70	29,48	29,39	29,35
3 000	47,44	45,37	44,55	44,22	44,08	44,03
4 000	63,25	60,49	59,40	58,96	58,78	58,70
5 000	79,06	75,61	74,25	73,70	73,47	73,37
6 000	94,88	90,73	89,10	88,44	88,16	88,05
7 000	110,69	105,85	103,95	103,17	102,86	102,72
8 000	126,50	120,97	118,80	117,91	117,55	117,40
9 000	142,31	136,09	133,65	132,65	132,24	132,07
10 000	158,12	151,21	148,49	147,39	146,93	146,74
15 000	237,18	226,81	222,74	221,08	220,40	220,11
20 000	316,24	302,41	296,98	294,78	293,86	293,48
25 000	395,30	378,01	371,23	368,48	367,33	366,85
30 000	474,36	453,61	445,47	442,16	440,79	440,22
35 000	553,42	529,21	519,72	515,85	514,26	513,59
40 000	632,48	604,81	593,96	589,55	587,72	586,96
45 000	711,54	680,41	668,21	663,24	661,19	660,33
50 000	790,60	756,02	742,45	736,93	734,65	733,70
60 000	948,72	907,22	890,94	884,32	881,58	880,44
70 000	1106,84	1058,42	1039,43	1031,70	1028,51	1027,18
80 000	1264,95	1209,62	1187,92	1179.09	1175,44	1173,92
90 000	1423,07	1360,82	1336,41	1326,47	1322,37	1320,66
100 000	1581,19	1512,03	1484,90	1473,86	1469,30	1467,40

	terms of loan (in years)					
Amount	1	2	3	4	5	10
500	45,80	24,92	18,04	14,65	12,65	8,96
1 000	91,60	49,84	36,07	29,29	25,30	17,91
2 000	183,20	99,68	72,13	58,57	50,60	35,82
3 000	274,79	149,52	108,20	87,86	75,90	53,72
4 000	366,39	199,36	144,26	117,14	101,20	71,63
5 000	457,99	249,20	180,33	146,42	126,50	89,53
6 000	549,58	299,04	216,39	175,71	151,79	107,44
7 000	641,18	348,88	252,46	204,99	177,09	125,35
8 000	732,78	398,72	288,52	234,27	202,39	143,25
9 000	824,37	448,56	324,59	263,56	227,69	161,16
10 000	915,97	498,40	360,65	292,84	252,99	179,06
15 000	1373,95	747,60	540,97	439,26	379,48	268,59
20 000	1831,94	996,79	721,30	585,68	505,97	356,12
25 000	2289,92	1245,99	901,62	732,09	632,46	447,65
30 000	2747,90	1495,19	1081,94	878,51	758,95	537,18
35 000	3205,89	1744,39	1262,27	1024,93	885,44	626,71
40 000	3663,87	1993,58	1442,59	1171,35	1011,93	716,24
45 000	4121,85	2242,78	1622,91	1317,76	1138,43	805,77
50 000	4579,84	2491,98	1803,23	1464,18	1264,92	895,30
60 000	5495,80	2990,37	2163,88	1757,02	1517,90	1074,36
70 000	6411,77	3488,77	2524,53	2049,85	1770,88	1253,42
80 000	7327,74	3987,16	2885,17	2342,69	2023,86	1432,48
90 000	8243,70	4485,56	3245,82	2635,52	2276,85	1611,54
100 000	9159,67	4983,95	3606,46	2928,36	2529,83	1790,59

Required monthly payment to refund a mortgage loan

18½%

Amount	terms of loan (in years)					
	15	20	25	30	35	40
500	7,99	7,65	7,52	7,47	7,45	7,44
1 000	15,98	15,30	15,04	14,93	14,89	14,87
2 000	31,96	30,60	30,07	29,86	29,77	29,74
3 000	47,94	45,90	45,11	44,79	44,66	44,60
4 000	63,92	61,20	60,14	59,72	59,54	59,47
5 000	79,90	76,50	75,18	74,64	74,43	74,34
6 000	95,87	91,80	90,21	89,57	89,31	89,20
7 000	111,85	107,09	105,25	104,50	104,20	104,07
8 000	127,83	122,39	120,28	119,43	119,08	118,94
9 000	143,81	137,69	135,31	134,36	133,96	133,80
10 000	159,79	152,99	150,35	149,28	148,85	148,67
15 000	239,68	229,48	225,52	223,92	223,27	223,00
20 000	319,57	305,97	300,69	298,56	297,69	297,34
25 000	399,46	382,47	375,86	373,20	372,12	371,67
30 000	479,35	458,96	451,03	447,84	446,54	446,00
35 000	559,25	535,45	526,21	522,48	520,96	520,33
40 000	639,14	611,94	601,38	597,12	595,38	594,67
45 000	719,03	688,43	676,55	671,76	669,80	669,00
50 000	798,92	764,93	751,72	746,40	744,23	743,33
60 000	958,70	917,91	902,06	895,68	893,07	892,00
70 000	1118,49	1070,90	1052,41	1044,96	1041,92	1040,66
80 000	1278,27	1223,88	1202,75	1194,24	1190,76	1189,33
90 000	1438,05	1376,86	1353,09	1343,52	1339,60	1338,00
100 000	1597,84	1529,85	1503,44	1492,80	1488,45	1486,66

Required monthly payment to refund a mortgage loan

Amount	terms of loan (in years)					
	1	2	3	4	5	10
500	45,86	24,98	18,10	14,71	12,72	9,03
1 000	91,71	49,96	36,19	29,41	25,43	18,06
2 000	183,42	99,91	72,37	58,81	50,85	36,12
3 000	275,13	149,86	108,55	88,22	76,28	54,17
4 000	366,83	199,81	144,73	117,62	101,70	72,23
5 000	458,54	249,76	180,91	147,03	127,13	90,28
6 000	550,25	299,71	217,09	176,43	152,55	108,34
7 000	641,95	349,67	253,27	205,84	177,98	126,39
8 000	733,66	399,62	289,45	235,24	203,40	144,45
9 000	825,37	449,57	325,63	264,65	228,82	162,50
10 000	917,08	499,52	361,81	294,05	254,25	180,56
15 000	1375,61	749,28	542,72	441,08	381,37	270,83
20 000	1834,15	999,04	723,62	588,10	508,49	361,11
25 000	2292,68	1248,80	904,53	735,12	635,62	451,38
30 000	2751,22	1498,55	1085,43	882,15	762,74	541,66
35 000	3209,75	1748,31	1266,34	1029,17	889,86	631,94
40 000	3668,29	1998,07	1447,24	1176,20	1016,98	722,21
45 000	4126,82	2247,83	1628,15	1323,22	1144,10	812,49
50 000	4585,36	2497,59	1809,05	1470,24	1271,23	902,76
60 000	5502,43	2997,10	2170,86	1764,29	1525,47	1083,32
70 000	6419,50	3496,62	2532,67	2058,34	1779,71	1263,87
80 000	7336,57	3996,13	2894,48	2352,39	2033,96	1444,42
90 000	8253,64	4495,65	3256,29	2646,43	2288,20	1624,97
100 000	9170,71	4995,17	3618,10	2940,48	2542,45	1805,52

Required monthly payment to refund a mortgage loan   18¾%

Amount	terms of loan (in years)					
	15	20	25	30	35	40
500	8,08	7,74	7,61	7,56	7,54	7,53
1 000	16,15	15,48	15,22	15,12	15,08	15,06
2 000	32,30	30,96	30,44	30,24	30,16	30,12
3 000	48,44	46,44	45,66	45,36	45,23	45,18
4 000	64,59	61,91	60,88	60,47	60,31	60,24
5 000	80,73	77,39	76,10	75,59	75,38	75,30
6 000	96,88	92,87	91,32	90,71	90,46	90,36
7 000	113,02	108,34	106,54	105,83	105,54	105,42
8 000	129,17	123,82	121,76	120,94	120,61	120,48
9 000	145,31	139,30	136,98	136,06	135,69	135,54
10 000	161,46	154,77	152,20	151,18	150,76	150,60
15 000	242,18	232,16	228,30	226,76	226,14	225,89
20 000	322,91	309,54	304,40	302,35	301,52	301,19
25 000	403,63	386,93	380,50	377,94	376,90	376,48
30 000	484,36	464,31	456,60	453,52	452,28	451,78
35 000	565,09	541,70	532,70	529,11	527,66	527,07
40 000	645,81	619,08	608,80	604,70	603,04	602,37
45 000	726,54	696,47	684,90	680,28	678,42	677,66
50 000	807,26	773,85	761,00	755,87	753,80	752,96
60 000	968,72	928,62	913,19	907,04	904,56	903,55
70 000	1130,17	1083,39	1065,39	1058,22	1055,32	1054,14
80 000	1291,62	1238,16	1217,59	1209,39	1206,08	1204,73
90 000	1453,07	1392,93	1369,79	1360,56	1356,83	1355,32
100 000	1614,52	1547,70	1521,99	1511,74	1507,59	1505,91

terms of loan (in years)

Amount	1	2	3	4	5	10
500	45,91	25,04	18,15	14,77	12,78	9,11
1 000	91,82	50,07	36,30	29,53	25,56	18,21
2 000	183,64	100,13	72,60	59,06	51,11	36,41
3 000	275,46	150,20	108,90	88,58	76,66	54,62
4 000	367,28	200,26	145,19	118,11	102,21	72,82
5 000	459,09	250,32	181,49	147,64	127,76	91,03
6 000	550,91	300,39	217,79	177,16	153,31	109,23
7 000	642,73	350,45	254,09	206,69	178,86	127,44
8 000	734,55	400,52	290,38	236,21	204,41	145,64
9 000	826,36	450,58	326,68	265,74	229,96	163,85
10 000	918,18	500,64	362,98	295,27	255,51	182,05
15 000	1377,27	750,96	544,47	442,90	383,27	273,08
20 000	1836,36	1001,28	725,95	590,53	511,02	364,10
25 000	2295,44	1251,60	907,44	738,16	638,78	455,13
30 000	2754,53	1501,92	1088,93	885,79	766,53	746,15
35 000	3213,62	1752,24	1270,42	1033,42	894,28	637,18
40 000	3672,71	2002,56	1451,90	1181,05	1022,04	728,20
45 000	4131,79	2252,87	1633,39	1328,68	1149,79	819,22
50 000	4590,88	2503,19	1814,88	1476,31	1277,55	910,25
60 000	5509,06	3003,83	2177,85	1771,57	1533,05	1092,30
70 000	6427,23	3504,47	2540,83	2066,83	1788,56	1274,35
80 000	7345,41	4005,11	2903,80	2362,10	2044,07	1456,40
90 000	8263,58	4505,74	3266,78	2657,36	2299,58	1638,44
100 000	9181,76	5006,38	3629,75	2952,62	2555,09	1820,49

Required monthly payment to refund a mortgage loan

19%

Amount	terms of loan (in years)					
	15	20	25	30	35	40
500	8,16	7,83	7,71	7,66	7,64	7,63
1 000	16,32	15,66	15,41	15,31	15,27	15,26
2 000	32,63	31,32	30,82	30,62	30,54	30,51
3 000	48,94	46,97	46,22	45,93	45,81	45,76
4 000	65,25	62,63	61,63	61,23	61,07	61,01
5 000	81,57	78,28	77,03	76,54	76,34	76,26
6 000	97,88	93,94	92,44	91,85	91,61	91,51
7 000	114,19	109,60	107,84	107,15	106,88	106,76
8 000	130,50	125,25	123,25	122,46	122,14	122,02
9 000	146,82	140,91	138,65	137,77	137,41	137,27
10 000	163,13	156,56	154,06	153,07	152,68	152,52
15 000	244,69	234,84	231,09	229,61	229,01	228,78
20 000	326,25	313,12	308,12	306,14	305,35	305,03
25 000	406,82	391,40	385,14	382,67	381,69	381,29
30 000	489,38	469,68	462,17	459,21	458,02	457,55
35 000	570,94	547,96	539,20	535,74	534,36	533,80
40 000	652,50	626,24	616,23	612,28	610,70	610,06
45 000	734,07	704,51	693,25	688,81	687,03	686,32
50 000	815,63	782,79	770,28	765,34	763,37	762,58
60 000	978,75	939,35	924,34	918,41	916,04	915,09
70 000	1141,88	1095,91	1078,39	1071,48	1068,72	1067,60
80 000	1305,00	1252,47	1232,45	1224,55	1221,39	1220,12
90 000	1468,13	1409,02	1386,50	1377,61	1374,06	1372,63
100 000	1631,25	1565,58	1540,56	1530,68	1526,73	1525,15

terms of loan (in years)

Amount	1	2	3	4	5	10
500	45,97	25,09	18,21	14,83	12,84	9,18
1 000	91,93	50,18	36,42	29,65	25,68	18,36
2 000	183,86	100,36	72,83	59,30	51,36	36,71
3 000	275,79	150,53	109,25	88,95	77,04	55,07
4 000	367,72	200,71	145,66	118,60	102,71	73,42
5 000	459,64	250,88	182,08	148,24	128,36	91,78
6 000	551,57	301,06	218,49	177,89	154,07	110,13
7 000	643,50	351,24	254,90	207,54	179,75	128,49
8 000	735,43	401,41	291,32	237,19	205,42	146,84
9 000	827,36	451,59	327,73	266,83	231,10	165,20
10 000	919,28	501,76	364,15	296,48	256,78	183,55
15 000	1378,92	752,64	546,22	444,72	385,17	275,33
20 000	1838,56	1003,52	728,29	592,96	513,55	367,10
25 000	2298,20	1254,40	910,36	741,20	641,94	458,88
30 000	2757,84	1505,28	1092,43	889,44	770,33	550,65
35 000	3217,48	1756,16	1274,50	1037,67	898,71	642,43
40 000	3677,12	2007,04	1456,57	1185,91	1027,10	734,20
45 000	4136,76	2257,92	1638,64	1334,15	1155,49	825,98
50 000	4596,40	2508,80	1820,71	1482,39	1283,88	917,75
60 000	5515,68	3010,56	2184,85	1778,87	1540,65	1101,30
70 000	6434,96	3512,32	2548,99	2075,34	1797,42	1284,85
80 000	7354,24	4014,08	2913,13	2371,82	2054,20	1468,40
90 000	8273,52	4515,84	3277,27	2668,30	2310,97	1651,95
100 000	9192,79	5017,60	3641,41	2964,77	2567,75	1835,50

Amount	\begin{tabular}{c}terms of loan (in years)\\15\end{tabular}	20	25	30	35	40
500	8,25	7,92	7,80	7,75	7,73	7,73
1 000	16,49	15,84	15,60	15,50	15,46	15,45
2 000	32,97	31,67	31,19	31,00	30,92	30,89
3 000	49,45	47,51	46,78	46,49	46,38	46,34
4 000	65,93	63,34	62,37	61,99	61,84	61,78
5 000	82,41	79,18	77,96	77,49	77,30	77,22
6 000	98,89	95,01	93,55	92,98	92,76	92,67
7 000	115,37	110,85	109,14	108,48	108,22	108,11
8 000	131,85	126,68	124,74	123,97	123,67	123,55
9 000	148,33	142,52	140,33	139,47	139,13	139,00
10 000	164,81	158,35	155,92	154,97	154,59	154,44
15 000	247,21	237,53	233,87	232,45	231,88	231,66
20 000	329,61	316,70	311,83	309,93	309,18	308,88
25 000	412,01	395,88	389,79	387,41	386,47	386,10
30 000	494,41	475,05	467,74	464,89	463,76	463,31
35 000	576,81	554,22	545,70	542,37	541,06	540,53
40 000	659,21	633,40	623,66	619,85	618,35	617,75
45 000	741,61	712,57	701,61	697,33	695,64	694,97
50 000	824,01	791,75	779,57	774,82	772,94	772,19
60 000	988,81	950,09	935,48	929,78	927,52	926,62
70 000	1153,61	1108,44	1091,40	1084,74	1082,11	1081,06
80 000	1318,41	1266,79	1247,31	1239,70	1236,69	1235,50
90 000	1483,21	1425,14	1403,22	1394,66	1391,28	1389,93
100 000	1648,01	1583,49	1559,13	1549,63	1545,87	1544,37

19½% Required monthly payment to refund a mortgage loan

terms of loan (in years)

Amount	1	2	3	4	5	10
500	46,02	25,15	18,27	14,89	12,91	9,26
1 000	92,04	50,29	36,54	29,77	25,81	18,51
2 000	184,08	100,58	73,07	59,54	51,61	37,02
3 000	276,12	150,87	109,60	89,31	77,42	55,52
4 000	368,16	201,16	146,13	119,08	103,22	74,03
5 000	460,20	251,45	182,66	148,85	129,03	92,53
6 000	552,23	301,73	219,19	178,62	154,83	111,04
7 000	644,27	352,02	255,72	208,39	180,63	129,54
8 000	736,31	402,31	292,25	238,16	206,44	148,05
9 000	828,35	452,60	328,78	267,93	232,24	166,55
10 000	920,39	502,89	365,31	297,70	258,05	185,06
15 000	1380,58	754,33	547,97	446,55	387,07	277,59
20 000	1840,77	1005,77	730,62	595,39	516,09	370,11
25 000	2300,96	1257,21	913,27	744,24	645,11	462,64
30 000	2761,15	1508,65	1095,93	893,09	774,13	555,17
35 000	3221,34	1760,09	1278,58	1041,93	903,15	647,69
40 000	3681,54	2011,53	1461,23	1190,78	1032,18	740,22
45 000	4141,73	2262,97	1643,89	1339,63	1161,20	832,75
50 000	4601,92	2514,41	1826,54	1488,47	1290,22	925,28
60 000	5522,30	3017,30	2191,85	1786,17	1548,26	1110,33
70 000	6442,68	3520,18	2557,16	2083,86	1806,30	1295,38
80 000	7363,07	4023,06	2922,46	2381,56	2064,35	1480,44
90 000	8283,45	4525,94	3287,77	2679,25	2322,39	1665,49
100 000	9203,83	5028,82	3653,08	2976,94	2580,43	1850,55

Required monthly payment to refund a mortgage loan   19½%

Amount	terms of loan (in years)					
	15	20	25	30	35	40
500	8,33	8,01	7,89	7,85	7,83	7,82
1 000	16,65	16,02	15,78	15,69	15,65	15,64
2 000	33,30	32,03	31,56	31,38	31,30	31,28
3 000	49,95	48,05	47,34	47,06	46,95	46,91
4 000	66,60	64,06	63,11	62,75	62,60	62,55
5 000	83,25	80,08	78,89	78,43	78,25	78,18
6 000	99,89	96,09	94,67	94,12	93,90	93,82
7 000	116,54	112,10	110,45	109,80	109,55	109,46
8 000	133,19	128,12	126,22	125,49	125,20	125,09
9 000	149,84	144,13	142,00	141,18	140,85	140,73
10 000	166,49	160,15	157,78	156,86	156,50	156,36
15 000	249,73	240,22	236,66	235,29	234,75	234,54
20 000	332,97	320,29	315,55	313,72	313,00	312,72
25 000	416,21	400,36	394,44	392,15	391,25	390,90
30 000	499,45	480,43	473,32	470,58	469,50	469,08
35 000	582,69	560,50	552,21	549,00	547,75	547,26
40 000	665,93	640,57	631,09	627,43	626,00	625,44
45 000	749,17	720,64	709,98	705,86	704,25	703,62
50 000	832,41	800,71	788,87	784,29	782,50	781,80
60 000	998,89	960,86	946,64	941,15	939,00	938,15
70 000	1165,37	1121,00	1104,41	1098,00	1095,50	1094,51
80 000	1331,86	1281,14	1262,18	1254,86	1252,00	1250,87
90 000	1498,34	1441,28	1419,96	1411,72	1408,49	1407,23
100 000	1664,82	1601,42	1577,73	1568,58	1564,99	1563,59

19¾% Required monthly payment to refund a mortgage loan

Amount	terms of loan (in years)					
	1	2	3	4	5	10
500	46,08	25,21	18,33	14,95	12,97	9,33
1 000	92,15	50,41	36,65	29,90	25,94	18,66
2 000	184,30	100,81	73,30	59,79	51,87	37,32
3 000	276,45	151,21	109,95	89,68	77,90	55,97
4 000	368,60	201,61	146,60	119,57	103,73	74,63
5 000	460,75	252,01	183,24	149,46	129,66	93,29
6 000	552,90	302,41	219,89	179,35	155,59	111,94
7 000	645,04	352,81	256,54	209,24	181,52	130,60
8 000	737,19	403,21	293,19	239,14	207,46	149,26
9 000	829,34	453,61	329,83	269,03	233,39	167,91
10 000	921,49	504,01	366,48	298,92	259,32	186,57
15 000	1382,23	756,01	549,72	448,37	388,97	279,85
20 000	1842,98	1008,01	732,96	597,83	518,63	373,13
25 000	2303,72	1260,02	916,19	747,29	648,29	466,41
30 000	2764,46	1512,02	1099,43	896,74	777,94	559,69
35 000	3225,20	1764,02	1282,67	1046,20	907,60	652,97
40 000	3685,95	2016,02	1465,91	1195,66	1037,26	746,26
45 000	4146,69	2268,03	1649,14	1345,11	1166,91	839,54
50 000	4607,43	2520,03	1832,38	1494,57	1296,57	932,82
60 000	5528,92	3024,03	2198,86	1793,48	1555,88	1119,38
70 000	6450,40	3528,04	2565,33	2092,39	18,15,20	1305,94
80 000	7371,89	4032,04	2931,81	2391,31	2074,51	1492,51
90 000	8293,38	4536,05	3298,28	2690,22	2333,82	1679,07
100 000	9214,86	5040,05	3664,76	2989,13	2593,14	1865,63

Required monthly payment to refund a mortgage loan 19¾%

Amount	15	20	25	30	35	40
500	8,41	8,10	7,99	7,94	7,93	7,92
1 000	16,82	16,20	15,97	15,88	15,85	15,83
2 000	33,64	32,39	31,93	31,76	31,69	31,66
3 000	50,45	48,59	47,89	47,63	47,53	47,49
4 000	67,27	64,78	63,86	63,51	63,37	63,32
5 000	84,09	80,97	79,82	79,38	79,21	79,14
6 000	100,90	97,17	95,78	95,26	95,08	94,97
7 000	117,72	113,36	111,75	111,13	110,89	110,80
8 000	134,54	129,56	127,71	127,01	126,73	126,63
9 000	151,35	145,75	143,67	142,88	142,57	142,46
10 000	168,17	161,94	159,64	158,76	158,42	158,28
15 000	252,25	242,91	239,45	238,13	237,62	237,42
20 000	336,34	323,88	319,27	317,51	316,83	316,56
25 000	420,42	404,85	399,09	396,88	396,03	395,70
30 000	504,50	485,82	478,90	476,26	475,24	471,84
35 000	588,58	566,79	558,72	555,64	554,44	553,98
40 000	672,67	647,76	638,54	635,01	633,65	633,12
45 000	756,75	728,73	718,35	714,39	712,85	712,26
50 000	840,63	809,69	798,17	793,76	792,06	791,40
60 000	1009,00	971,63	957,80	952,51	950,47	949,67
70 000	1177,16	1133,57	1117,43	1111,27	1108,88	1107,95
80 000	1345,33	1295,51	1277,07	1270,02	1267,29	1266,23
90 000	1513,49	1457,45	1436,70	1428,77	1425,70	1424,51
00 000	1681,66	1619,38	1596,33	1587,52	1584,11	1582,79

terms of loan (in years)

20% Required monthly payment to refund a mortgage loan

Amount	terms of loan (in years)					
	1	2	3	4	5	10
500	46,13	25,26	18,39	15,01	13,03	9,41
1 000	92,26	50,52	36,77	30,02	26,06	18,81
2 000	184,52	101,03	73,53	60,03	52,12	37,62
3 000	276,78	151,54	110,30	90,04	78,18	56,43
4 000	369,04	202,06	147,06	120,06	104,24	75,23
5 000	461,30	252,57	183,83	150,07	130,30	94,04
6 000	553,56	303,08	220,59	180,08	156,36	112,85
7 000	645,82	353,59	257,36	210,10	182,41	131,66
8 000	738,08	404,11	294,12	240,11	208,47	150,46
9 000	830,33	454,62	330,88	270,12	234,53	169,27
10 000	922,59	505,13	367,65	300,14	260,59	188,08
15 000	1383,89	757,70	551,47	450,20	390,88	282,12
20 000	1845,18	1010,26	735,29	600,27	521,18	376,15
25 000	2306,48	1262,82	919,12	750,34	651,47	470,19
30 000	2767,77	1515,39	1102,94	900,40	781,76	564,23
35 000	3229,06	1767,95	1286,76	1050,47	972,05	658,27
40 000	3690,36	2020,52	1470,58	1200,54	1042,35	752,30
45 000	4151,65	2273,08	1654,40	1350,60	1172,64	846,34
50 000	4612,95	2525,64	1838,23	1500,67	1302,93	940,38
60 000	5535,54	3030,77	2205,87	1800,80	1563,52	1128,45
70 000	6458,13	3535,90	2573,52	2100,94	18,24,11	1316,53
80 000	7380,71	4041,03	2941,16	2401,07	2084,69	1504,60
90 000	8303,30	4546,15	3308,80	2701,20	2345,28	1692,68
100 000	9225,89	5051,28	3676,45	3001,33	2605,86	1880,75

Required monthly payment to refund a mortgage loan   **20%**

terms of loan (in years)

Amount	15	20	25	30	35	40
500	8,50	8,19	8,08	8,04	8,02	8,01
1 000	16,99	16,38	16,15	16,07	16,04	16,02
2 000	33.98	32,75	32,30	32,13	32.07	32,04
3 000	50,96	49,13	48,45	48,20	48,10	48,06
4 000	67,95	65,50	64,60	64.26	64,13	64,08
5 000	84.93	81,87	80,75	80,33	80,17	80.10
6 000	101,92	98,25	96,90	96,39	96,20	96,12
7 000	118.90	114,62	113,05	112,46	112,23	112,14
8 000	135,89	130,99	129,20	128,52	128,26	128,16
9 000	152,87	147,37	145,35	144,39	144,29	144,18
10 000	169,86	163,74	161,50	160,65	160,33	160,20
15 000	254,78	245,61	242,25	240,97	240.49	240,30
20 000	339,71	327,48	322,99	321,30	320,65	320,40
25 000	424,64	409,35	403,74	401,62	400,81	400,50
30 000	509,56	491,21	484,49	481,94	480,97	480,60
35 000	594,49	573,08	565,24	562,27	561,13	560,69
40 000	679,42	654,95	645,98	642,59	641,29	640,79
45 000	764,34	736,82	726,73	722,91	721,45	720,89
50 000	849,27	818,69	807,48	803,24	801,61	800,99
60 000	1019,12	982,42	968,97	963,88	961,94	961,19
70 000	1188,97	1146,16	1130,47	1124,53	1122,26	1121,38
80 000	1358,83	1309,90	1291,96	1285,18	1282,58	1281,58
90 000	1528,68	1473,63	1453,45	1445,82	1442,90	1441,78
100 000	1698,53	1637,37	1614,95	1606,47	1603,22	1601,97

20¼% Required monthly payment to refund a mortgage loan

Amount	terms of loan (in years)					
	1	2	3	4	5	10
500	46,19	25,32	18,45	15,07	13,10	9,48
1 000	92,37	50,63	36,89	30,14	26,19	18,96
2 000	184,74	101,26	73,77	60,28	52,38	37,92
3 000	277,11	151,88	110,65	90,41	78,56	56,88
4 000	369,48	202,51	147,53	120,55	104,75	75,84
5 000	461,85	253,13	184,81	150,68	130,94	94,80
6 000	554,22	303,76	221,29	180,82	157,12	113,76
7 000	646,59	354,38	258,17	210,95	183,31	132,72
8 000	738,96	405,01	295,06	241,09	209,49	151,68
9 000	831,33	455,63	331,94	271,22	235,68	170,64
10 000	923,70	506,26	368,82	301,36	261,87	189,60
15 000	1385,54	759,38	553,23	452,04	392,80	284,39
20 000	1847,39	1012,51	737,63	602,71	523,73	379,19
25 000	2309,23	1265,63	922,04	753,39	654,66	473,98
30 000	2771,08	1518,76	1106,45	904,07	785,59	568,78
35 000	3232,92	1771,88	1290,85	1054,75	916,52	663,57
40 000	3694,97	2025,01	1475,26	1205,42	1047,45	758,37
45 000	4156,61	2278,13	1659,67	1356,10	1178,38	853,16
50 000	4618,46	2531,26	1844,08	1506,78	1309,31	947,96
60 000	5542,15	3037,51	2212,89	1808,13	1571,17	1137,55
70 000	6465,84	3543,76	2581,70	2101,49	1833,03	1327,14
80 000	7389,53	4050,01	2950,52	2410,84	2094,89	1516,73
90 000	8313,22	4556,26	3319,33	2712,20	2356,75	1706,32
100 000	9236,92	5062,51	3688,15	3013,55	2618,61	1895,91

Amount	terms of loan (in years)					
	15	20	25	30	35	40
500	8,58	8,28	8,17	8,13	8,12	8,11
1 000	17,16	16,56	16,34	16,26	16,23	16,22
2 000	34,31	33,11	32,68	32,51	32,45	32,43
3 000	51,47	49,67	49,01	48,77	48,67	48,64
4 000	68,62	66,22	65,35	65,02	64,90	64,85
5 000	85,78	82,77	81,68	81,28	81,12	81,06
6 000	102,93	99,33	98,02	97,53	97,34	97,27
7 000	120,09	115,88	114,35	113,78	113,57	114,48
8 000	137,24	132,43	130,69	130,04	129,79	129,70
9 000	154,39	148,99	147,03	146,29	146,01	145,91
10 000	171,55	165,54	163,36	162,55	162,24	162,12
15 000	257,32	248,31	245,04	243,82	243,35	243,18
20 000	343,09	331,08	326,72	325,09	324,47	324,23
25 000	428,86	413,85	408,40	406,36	405,58	405,29
30 000	514,64	496,62	490,07	487,63	486,70	486,35
35 000	600,41	579,38	571,75	568,90	567,82	567,40
40 000	686,18	662,15	653,43	650,17	648,93	648,46
45 000	771,95	744,92	735,11	731,44	730,05	729,52
50 000	857,72	827,69	816,79	812,71	811,16	810,58
60 000	1029,27	993,23	980,14	975,25	973,39	972,69
70 000	1200,81	1158,76	1143,50	1137,79	1135,63	1134,80
80 000	1372,35	1324,30	1306,86	1300,33	1297,86	1296,92
90 000	1543,90	1489,84	1470,21	1462,87	1460,09	1459,03
00 000	1715,44	1655,37	1633,57	1625,41	1622,32	1621,15

20½% Required monthly payment to refund a mortgage loan

terms of loan (in years)

Amount	1	2	3	4	5	10
500	46,24	25,37	18,50	15,13	13,16	9,56
1 000	92,48	50,74	37,00	30,26	26,32	19,12
2 000	184,96	101,48	74,00	60,52	52,63	38,23
3 000	277,44	152,22	111,00	90,78	78,95	57,34
4 000	369,92	202,95	148,00	121,04	105,26	76,45
5 000	462,40	253,69	185,00	151,29	131,57	95,56
6 000	554,88	304,43	222,00	181,55	157,89	114,67
7 000	647,36	355,17	258,99	211,81	184,20	133,78
8 000	739,84	405,90	295,99	242,07	210,51	152,89
9 000	832,32	456,64	332,99	272,33	236,83	172,00
10 000	924,80	507,38	369,99	302,58	263,14	191,11
15 000	1387,19	761,07	554,98	453,87	394,71	286,67
20 000	1849,59	1014,75	739,98	605,16	526,28	382,22
25 000	23i1,99	1268,44	924,97	756,45	657,85	477,78
30 000	2774,38	1522,13	1109,96	907,74	789,42	573,33
35 000	3236,78	1775,82	1294,95	1059,03	920,99	668,89
40 000	3699,18	2029,50	1479,95	1210,32	1052,55	764,44
45 000	4161,57	2283,19	1664,94	1361,61	1!84,12	860,00
50 000	4623,97	2536,88	1849,93	1512,90	1315,69	955,55
60 000	5548,76	3044,25	2219,92	1815,47	1578,83	1146,66
70 000	6473,56	3551,63	2589,90	2118,05	1841,97	1337,77
80 000	7398,35	4059,00	2959,89	2420,63	2105,10	1528,88
90 000	8323,14	4566,38	3329,87	2723,21	23,68,24	1719,99
100 000	9247,94	5073,75	3699,86	3025,79	2631,38	1911,10

Required monthly payment to refund a mortgage loan

20½%

Amount	terms of loan (in years)					
	15	20	25	30	35	40
500	8,67	8,37	8,27	8,23	8,21	8,21
1 000	17,33	16,74	16,53	16,45	16,42	16,41
2 000	34,65	33,47	33,05	32,89	32,83	32,81
3 000	51,98	50,21	49,57	49,34	49,25	49,21
4 000	69.30	66,94	66,09	65,78	65,66	65,62
5 000	86,62	83,67	82,61	82,22	82,08	82,02
6 000	103,95	100,41	99,14	98,67	98,49	98,42
7 000	121,27	117,14	115,66	115,11	114,90	114,83
8 000	138,60	133,88	132,18	131,55	131,32	131,23
9 000	155,92	150,61	148,70	148,00	147,73	147,63
10 000	173,24	167,34	165,22	164,44	164,15	164,04
15 000	259,86	251,01	247,83	247,66	246,22	246,05
20 000	346,48	334,68	330,44	328,87	328,29	328,07
25 000	433,10	418,35	413,05	411,09	410,36	410,08
30 000	519,72	502,02	495,66	493,31	492,43	492,10
35 000	606,34	585,69	578,27	575,53	574,50	574,11
40 000	692,96	669,36	660,88	657,74	656,57	656,13
45 000	779,58	753,03	743,49	739,96	738,64	738,14
50 000	866,19	836,70	826,10	822,18	820,71	820,16
60 000	1039,43	1004,04	991,32	986,61	984,85	984,19
70 000	1212,67	1171,38	1156,54	1151,05	1148,99	1148,22
80 000	1385,91	1338,72	1321,76	1315,48	1313,13	1312,25
90 000	1559,15	1506,06	1486,98	1479,92	1477,27	1476,28
100 000	1732,38	1673,40	1652,20	1644,35	1641,41	1640,31

20¾% Required monthly payment to refund a mortgage loan

terms of loan (in years)

Amount	1	2	3	4	5	10
500	46,30	25,43	18,56	15,20	13,23	9,64
1 000	92,59	50,85	37,12	30,39	26,45	19,27
2 000	185,18	101,70	74,24	60,77	52,89	38,53
3 000	277,77	152,55	111,35	91,15	79,33	57,79
4 000	370,36	203,40	148,47	121,53	105,77	77,06
5 000	462,95	254,25	185,58	151,91	132,21	96,32
6 000	555,54	305,10	222,70	182,29	158,65	115,58
7 000	648,13	355,95	259,81	212,67	185,10	134,85
8 000	740,72	406,80	296,93	243,05	211,54	154,11
9 000	833,31	457,65	334,05	273,43	237,98	173,37
10 000	925,90	508,50	371,16	303,81	264,42	192,64
15 000	1388,85	762,75	556,74	455,71	396,63	288,95
20 000	1851,80	1017,00	742,32	607,61	528,84	385,27
25 000	2314,74	1271,25	926,90	759,51	661,04	481,59
30 000	2777,69	1525,50	1113,48	911,41	793,25	577,90
35 000	3240,64	1779,75	1299,05	1063,32	925,46	674,22
40 000	3703,59	2034,00	1484,63	1215,22	1057,67	770,54
45 000	4166,53	2288,25	1670,21	1367,12	1189,88	866,85
50 000	4629,48	2542,50	1855,79	1519,02	1322,08	963,17
60 000	5555,38	3051,00	2226,95	1822,82	1586,50	1155,80
70 000	6481,27	3559,50	2598,10	2126,63	1850,92	1348,43
80 000	7407,17	4068,00	2969,26	2430,43	2115,33	1541,07
90 000	8333,06	4576,49	3340,42	2734,23	2379,75	1733,70
100 000	9258,96	5084,99	3711,57	3038,03	2644,16	1926,33

Required monthly payment to refund a mortgage loan 20¾%

Amount	terms of loan (in years)					
	15	20	25	30	35	40
500	8,75	8,46	8,36	8,32	8,31	8,30
1 000	17,50	16,92	16,71	16,64	16,61	16,60
2 000	34,99	33,83	33,42	33,27	33,21	33,19
3 000	52,49	50,75	50,13	49,90	49,82	49,79
4 000	69,98	67,66	66,84	66,54	66,42	66,38
5 000	87,47	84,58	83,55	83,17	83,03	82,98
6 000	104,97	101,49	100,26	99,80	99,63	99,57
7 000	122,46	118,41	116,96	116,43	116,24	116,17
8 000	139,95	135,32	133,67	133,07	132,84	132,76
9 000	157,45	152,24	150,38	149,70	149,45	149,36
10 000	174,74	169,15	167,09	166,33	166,05	165,95
15 000	262,41	253,72	250,63	249,50	249,08	248,92
20 000	349,88	338,29	334,17	332,66	332,10	331,89
25 000	437,34	422,87	417,71	415,83	415,13	414,87
30 000	524,81	507,44	501,26	498,99	498,15	497,84
35 000	612,28	592,01	584,80	582,15	581,18	580,81
40 000	699,75	676,78	668,34	665,32	664,20	663,78
45 000	787,21	761,16	751,88	748,48	747,22	746,76
50 000	874,68	845,73	835,42	831,65	830,25	829,73
60 000	1049,62	1014,87	1002,51	997,98	996,30	995,67
70 000	1224,55	1184,02	1169,59	1164,30	1162,35	1161,62
80 000	1399,49	1353,16	1336,67	1330,63	1328,40	1327,56
90 000	1574,42	1522,31	1503,76	1496,96	1494,44	1493,51
100 000	1749,36	1691,45	1670,84	1663,29	1660,49	1659,45

21%

Required monthly payment to refund a mortgage loan

terms of loan (in years)

Amount	1	2	3	4	5	10
500	46,35	25,49	18,62	15,26	13,29	9,71
1 000	92,70	50,97	37,24	30,51	26,57	19,42
2 000	185,40	101,93	74,47	61,01	53,14	38,84
3 000	278,10	152,89	111,70	91,51	79,71	58,25
4 000	370,80	203,85	148,94	122,02	106,28	77,67
5 000	463,50	254,82	186,17	152,52	132,85	97,08
6 000	556,20	305,78	223,40	183,02	159,42	116,50
7 000	648,90	356,74	260,64	213,53	185,99	135,92
8 000	741,60	407,70	297,87	244,03	212,56	155,33
9 000	834,30	458,67	335,10	274,53	239,13	174,75
10 000	927,00	509,63	372,33	305,03	265,70	194,16
15 000	1390,50	764,44	558,50	457,55	398,55	291,24
20 000	1854,00	1019,25	744,66	610,06	531,40	388,32
25 000	2317,50	1274,06	930,83	762,58	664,25	485,40
30 000	2781,00	1528,88	1116,99	915,09	797,10	582,48
35 000	3244,49	1783,69	1303,16	1067,61	929,94	679,56
40 000	3707,99	2038,50	1489,32	1220,12	1062,79	776,64
45 000	4171,49	2293,31	1675,49	1372,64	1195,64	873,72
50 000	4634,99	2548,12	1861,65	1525,15	1328,49	970,80
60 000	5561,99	3057,75	2233,98	1930,18	1594,19	1164,96
70 000	6488,98	3567,37	2606,31	2135,21	1859,88	1359,12
80 000	7415,98	4076,99	2978,64	2440,24	2125,58	1553,28
90 000	8342,98	4586,62	3350,97	2745,27	2391,28	1747,44
100 000	9269,97	5096,24	3723,30	3050,30	2656,97	1941,60

Required monthly payment to refund a mortgage loan
21%

Amount	terms of loan (in years)					
	15	20	25	30	35	40
500	8,84	8,55	8,45	8,42	8,40	8,40
1 000	17,67	17,10	16,90	16,83	16,80	16,79
2 000	35,33	34,20	33,79	33,65	33,60	33,58
3 000	53,00	51,29	50,69	50,47	50,39	50,36
4 000	70,66	68,39	67,58	67,29	67,19	67,15
5 000	88,32	85,48	84,48	84,12	83,98	83,93
6 000	105,99	102,58	101,37	100,94	100,78	100,72
7 000	123,65	119,67	118,27	117,76	117,57	117,51
8 000	141,31	136,77	135,16	134,58	134,37	134,29
9 000	158,98	153,86	152,06	151,40	151,17	151,08
10 000	176,64	170,96	168,95	168,23	167,96	167,86
15 000	264,96	256,43	253,43	252,34	251,94	251,79
20 000	353,28	341,91	337,90	336,45	335,92	335,72
25 000	441,60	427,38	422,38	420,56	419,90	419,65
30 000	529,91	512,86	506,85	504,67	503,87	503,58
35 000	618,23	598,34	591,32	588,78	587,85	587,51
40 000	706,55	683,81	675,80	672,89	671,83	671,44
45 000	794,87	769,29	760,27	757,00	755,81	755,37
50 000	883,19	854,76	844,75	841,12	839,79	839,30
60 000	1059,82	1025,72	1013,70	1009,34	1007,74	1007,15
70 000	1236,46	1196,67	1182,64	1177,56	1175,70	1175,01
80 000	1413,10	1367,62	1351,59	1345,78	1343,65	1342,87
90 000	1589,73	1538,57	1520,54	1514,00	1511,61	1510,73
100 000	1766,37	1709,52	1689,49	1682,23	1679,57	1678,59

133

21½% Required monthly payment to refund a mortgage loan

Amount	terms of loan (in years)					
	1	2	3	4	5	10
500	46,46	25,60	18,74	15,38	13,42	9,87
1 000	92,92	51,19	37,47	30,75	26,83	19,73
2 000	185,84	102,38	74,94	61,50	53,66	39,45
3 000	278,76	153,57	112,41	92,25	80,48	59,17
4 000	371,68	204,75	149,88	123,00	107,31	78,89
5 000	464,60	255,94	187,34	153,75	134,14	98,62
6 000	557,52	307,13	224,81	184,50	160,96	118,34
7 000	650,44	358,32	262,28	215,25	187,79	138,06
8 000	743,36	409,50	299,75	245,99	214,62	157,78
9 000	836,28	460,69	337,22	276,74	241,44	177,51
10 000	929,20	511,88	374,68	307,49	268,27	197,23
15 000	1393,80	767,81	562,02	461,24	402,40	295,84
20 000	1858,40	1023,75	749,36	614,98	536,53	394,45
25 000	2323,00	1279,69	936,70	768,72	670,67	493,06
30 000	2787,60	1535,62	1124,04	922,47	804,80	591,67
35 000	3252,20	1791,56	1311,38	1076,21	938,93	690,28
40 000	3716,80	2047,50	1498,72	1229,95	1073,06	788,89
45 000	4181,40	2303,43	1686,06	1383,70	1207,20	887,51
50 000	4646,00	2559,37	1873,40	1537,44	1341,33	986,12
60 000	5575,20	3071,24	2248,08	1844,93	1609,59	1183,34
70 000	6504,40	3583,12	2622,75	2152,41	1877,86	1380,56
80 000	7433,60	4094,99	2997,43	2459,90	2146,12	1577,78
90 000	8362,79	4606,86	3372,11	2767,39	2414,39	1775,01
100 000	9291,99	5118,74	3746,79	3074,87	2682,65	1972,23

Amount	terms of loan (in years)					
	15	20	25	30	35	40
500	9,01	8.73	8,64	8,61	8,59	8,59
1 000	18,01	17,46	17,27	17,21	17,18	17,17
2 000	36,01	34,92	34,54	34,41	34,36	34,34
3 000	54,02	52,38	51,81	51,61	51,54	51,51
4 000	72,02	69,83	69,08	68,81	68,71	68,68
5 000	90,03	87,29	86,34	86,01	85,89	85,85
6 000	108,03	104,75	103,61	103,21	103,07	103,01
7 000	126,04	122,20	120,88	120,41	120,24	120,18
8 000	144,04	139,66	138,15	137,61	137,42	137,35
9 000	162,05	157,12	155,42	154,81	154,60	154,52
10 000	180,05	174,58	172,66	172,01	171,77	171,69
15 000	270,08	261,86	259,02	258,02	257,66	257,53
20 000	360,10	349,15	345,36	344,02	343,54	343,37
25 000	450,12	436,43	431,70	430,02	429,42	429,21
30 000	540,15	523,72	518,04	516,03	515,31	515,05
35 000	630,17	611,00	604,38	602,03	601,19	600,89
40 000	720,19	698,29	690,72	688,03	687,07	686,73
45 000	810,22	785,57	777,06	774,04	772,96	772,57
50 000	900,24	872,86	863,40	860,04	858,84	858,41
60 000	1080,29	1047,43	1036,08	1032,05	1030,61	1030,09
70 000	1260,33	1222,00	1208,76	1204,06	1202,37	1201,77
80 000	1440,38	1396,57	1381,44	1376,06	1374,14	1373,45
90 000	1620,43	1571,14	1554,11	1548,07	1545,91	1545,13
100 000	1800,47	1745,71	1726,79	1720,08	1717,67	1716,81

22% Required monthly payment to refund a mortgage loan

terms of loan (in years)

Amount	1	2	3	4	5	10
500	46,57	25,71	18,86	15,50	13,55	10,02
1 000	93,14	51,42	37,71	31,00	27,09	20,03
2 000	186,28	102,83	75,41	62,00	54,17	40,06
3 000	279,42	154,24	113,11	92,99	81,26	60,09
4 000	372,56	205,65	150,82	123,99	108,34	80,12
5 000	465,70	257,07	188,52	154,98	135,43	100,15
6 000	558,84	308,48	226,22	185,98	162,51	120,18
7 000	651,98	359,89	263,93	216,97	189,59	140,21
8 000	745,12	411,30	301,63	247,97	216,68	160,24
9 000	838,26	462,72	339,33	278,96	243,76	180,27
10 000	931,40	514,13	377,04	309,96	270,85	200,30
15 000	1397,10	771,19	565,55	464,93	406,27	300,45
20 000	1862,80	1028,25	754,07	619,91	541,69	400,60
25 000	2328,50	1285,32	942,58	774,88	677,11	500,75
30 000	2794,20	1542,38	1131,10	929,86	812,53	600,90
35 000	3259,90	1799,44	1319,61	1084,83	947,95	701,05
40 000	3725,60	2056,50	1508,13	1239,81	1083,37	801,20
45 000	4191,30	2313,57	1696,64	1394,78	1218,79	901,35
50 000	4657,00	2570,63	1885,16	1549,76	1354,21	1001,50
60 000	5588,40	3084,75	2262,19	1859,71	1625,05	1201,80
70 000	6519,80	3598,88	2639,22	2169,66	1895,89	1402,10
80 000	7451,20	4113,00	3016,25	2479,61	2166,73	1602,39
90 000	8382,60	4627,13	3393,28	2789,56	2437,57	1802,69
100 000	9314,00	5141,25	3770,31	3099,51	2708,41	2002,99

136

Required monthly payment to refund a mortgage loan **22%**

terms of loan (in years)

Amount	15	20	25	30	35	40
500	9,18	8,91	8,83	8,79	8,78	8,78
1 000	18,35	17,82	17,65	17,58	17,56	17,55
2 000	36,70	35,64	35,29	35,16	35,12	35,10
3 000	55,05	53,46	52,93	52,74	52,68	52,65
4 000	73,39	71,28	70,57	70,32	70,23	70,20
5 000	91,74	89,10	88,21	87 90	87,79	87,75
6 000	110,09	106,92	105,85	105,48	105,35	105,30
7 000	128,43	124,74	123,49	123,06	122,91	122,85
8 000	146,78	142,56	141,13	140,64	140,46	140,40
9 000	165,13	160,38	158,77	158,22	158,02	157,95
10 000	183,47	178,20	176,42	175,80	175,58	175,50
15 000	275,21	267,30	264,62	263,69	263,36	263,25
20 000	366,94	356,40	352,83	351,59	351,15	351,00
25 000	458,68	445,50	441,03	439,48	438,94	438,75
30 000	550,41	534,59	529,24	527,38	526,72	526,49
35 000	642,15	623,69	617,44	615,27	614,51	614,24
40 000	733,88	712,79	705,65	703,17	702,30	701,99
45 000	825,62	801,89	793,85	791,06	790,08	789,74
50 000	917,35	890,99	882,06	878,96	877,87	877,49
60 000	1100,82	1069,18	1058,47	1054,75	1053,44	1052,98
70 000	1284,29	1247,38	1234,88	1230,54	1229,01	1228,48
80 000	1467,76	1425,58	1411,29	1406,33	1404,59	1403,98
90 000	1651,23	1603,77	1587,70	1582,12	1580,16	1579,47
100 000	1834,70	1781,97	1764,11	1757,91	1755,73	1754,97

Required monthly payment to refund a mortgage loan

Amount	terms of loan (in years)					
	1	2	3	4	5	10
500	46,68	25,82	18,97	15,63	13,68	10,17
1 000	93,36	51,64	37,94	31,25	27,35	20,34
2 000	186,72	103,28	75,88	62,49	54,69	40,68
3 000	280,08	154,92	113,82	93,73	82,03	61,02
4 000	373,44	206,56	151,76	124,97	109,37	81,36
5 000	466,80	258,19	189,70	156,22	136,72	101,70
6 000	560,16	309,83	227,64	187,46	164,06	122,04
7 000	653,52	361,47	265,58	218,70	191,40	142,38
8 000	746,88	413,11	303,51	249,94	218,74	162,72
9 000	840,24	464,74	341,45	281,18	246,09	183,05
10 000	933,60	516,38	379,39	312,43	273,43	203,39
15 000	1400,40	774,57	569,09	468,64	410,14	305,09
20 000	1867,20	1032,76	758,78	624,85	546,85	406,78
25 000	2334,00	1290,95	948,47	781,06	683,57	508,47
30 000	2800,80	1549,14	1138,17	937,27	820,28	610,17
35 000	3267,60	1807,33	1327,86	1093,48	956,99	711,86
40 000	3734,40	2065,51	1517,55	1249,69	1093,70	813,56
45 000	4201,20	2323,70	1707,25	1405,90	1230,42	915,25
50 000	4608,00	2581,89	1896,94	1562,11	1367,13	1016,94
60 000	5601,60	3098,27	2276,33	1874,53	1640,55	1220,33
70 000	6535,20	3614,65	2655,71	2186,95	1913,98	1423,72
80 000	7468,80	4131,02	3035,10	2499,37	2187,40	1627,11
90 000	8402,40	4647,40	3414,49	2811,79	2460,83	1830,50
100 000	9336,00	5163,78	3793,88	3124,21	2734,25	2033,88

Amount	terms of loan (in years)					
	15	20	25	30	35	40
500	9,35	9,10	9,01	8,98	8,97	8,97
1 000	18,70	18,19	18.02	17,96	17,94	17,94
2 000	37,39	36,37	36,03	35,92	35,88	35,87
3 000	56,08	54,55	54,05	53,88	53,82	53,80
4 000	74,77	72,74	72.06	71,83	71,75	71,73
5 000	93,46	90,92	90,08	89,79	89,69	89,66
6 000	112,15	109,10	108,09	107,75	107,63	107,59
7 000	130,84	127,28	126,11	125,70	125,57	125,52
8 000	149,53	145,47	144,12	143,66	143,50	143,45
9 000	168,22	163,65	162,13	161,62	161,44	161.38
10 000	186,91	181,83	180,15	179,58	179,38	179,31
15 000	280,36	272,75	270,22	269,36	269,07	268,96
20 000	373,81	363,66	360,29	359,15	358,75	358,62
25 000	467,26	454,57	450,36	448,93	448,44	448,27
30 000	560,71	545,49	540,43	538,72	538,13	537.92
35 000	654,16	636,40	630,51	628,50	627,81	627,58
40 000	747,61	727,31	720,58	718,29	717,50	717,23
45 000	841,07	818,23	810,65	808,07	807,19	806,88
50 000	934,52	909,14	900,72	897,86	896,87	896,54
60 000	1121,42	1090,97	1080,86	1077,43	1076,25	1075.84
70 000	1308,32	1272,80	1261,01	1257,00	1255,62	1255,15
80 000	1495,22	1454,62	1441,15	1436,57	1434,99	1434,45
90 000	1682,13	1636,45	1621,29	1616,14	1614,37	1613,76
100 000	1869,03	1818,28	1801,43	1795,71	1793,74	1793,07

Amount	terms of loan (in years)					
	1	2	3	4	5	10
500	46,79	25,94	19,09	15,75	13,81	10,33
1 000	93,58	51,87	38.18	31,49	27,61	20,65
2 000	187,16	103,73	76,35	62,98	55,21	41,30
3 000	280,74	155,59	114,53	94,47	82,81	61,95
4 000	374,32	207,46	152,70	125,96	110,41	82,60
5 000	467,90	259,32	190,88	157,45	138,01	103,25
6 000	561,48	311,18	229,05	188,94	165,61	123,90
7 000	655,06	363,05	267,23	220,43	193,22	144,55
8 000	748,64	414,91	305,40	251,92	220,82	165,20
9 000	842,22	466,77	343,58	283,41	248,42	165,85
10 000	935,80	518,64	381,75	314,90	276,02	206,49
15 000	1403,70	777,95	572,63	472,35	414,03	309,74
20 000	1871,60	1037,27	763,50	629,80	552,04	412,98
25 000	2339,50	1296,58	954,37	787,24	690,05	516,23
30 000	2807,40	1555,90	1145,25	944,29	828,05	619,47
35 000	3275,30	1815,21	1336,12	1102,14	966,06	722,72
40 000	3743,19	2074,53	1526,99	1259,59	1104,07	825,96
45 000	4211,09	2333,85	1717,87	1417,03	1242,08	929,21
50 000	4678,99	2593,16	1908,74	1574,48	1380,09	1032,45
60 000	5614,79	3111,79	2290,49	1889,38	1656,10	1238,94
70 000	6550,59	3630,42	2672,23	2204,27	1932,12	1445,43
80 000	7486,38	4149,05	3053,98	2519,17	2208,13	1651,92
90 000	8422,18	4667,69	3435,73	2834,06	2484,15	1858,41
100 000	9357,98	5186,32	3817,48	3148,96	2760,17	2064,90

Required monthly payment to refund a mortgage loan

23%

Amount	terms of loan (in years)					
	15	20	25	30	35	40
500	9,52	9,28	9,20	9,17	9,16	9,16
1 000	19,04	18,55	18,39	18,34	18,32	18,32
2 000	38,07	37,10	36,78	36,67	36,64	36,63
3 000	57,11	55,64	55,17	55,01	54,96	54,94
4 000	76,14	74,19	73,56	73,34	73,27	73,25
5 000	95,18	92,74	91,94	91,68	91,59	91,56
6 000	114,21	111,28	110,33	110,01	109,91	109,87
7 000	133,25	129,83	128,72	128,35	128,22	128,18
8 000	152,28	148,38	147,11	146,68	146,54	146,49
9 000	171,32	166,92	165,49	165,02	164,86	164,80
10 000	190,35	185,47	183,88	183,35	183,17	183,11
15 000	285,52	278,20	275,82	275,03	274,76	274,67
20 000	380,70	370,93	367,76	366,70	366,34	366,22
25 000	475,87	463,66	459,69	458,37	457,93	457,78
30 000	571,04	556,40	551,63	550,05	549,51	549,33
35 000	666,21	649,13	643,57	641,72	641,10	640,89
40 000	761,39	741,86	735,51	733,39	732,68	732,44
45 000	856,56	834,59	827,44	825,07	824,27	824,00
50 000	951,73	927,32	919,38	916,74	915,85	915,55
60 000	1142,08	1112,79	1103,26	1100,09	1099,02	1098,66
70 000	1332,42	1298,25	1287,13	1283,43	1282,19	1281,77
80 000	1522,77	1483,71	1471,01	1466,78	1465,36	1464,88
90 000	1713,12	1669,18	1654,88	1650,13	1648,53	1647,99
100 000	1903,46	1854,64	1838,76	1833,47	1831,70	1831,10

23½% Required monthly payment to refund a mortgage loan

terms of loan (in years)

Amount	1	2	3	4	5	10
500	46,90	26,05	19,21	15,87	13,94	10,49
1 000	93,80	52,09	38,42	31,74	27,87	20,97
2 000	187,60	104,18	76,83	63,48	55,73	41,93
3 000	281,40	156,27	115,24	95,22	63,59	62,89
4 000	375,20	208,36	153,65	126,96	111,45	83,85
5 000	469,00	260,45	192,06	158,69	139,31	104,81
6 000	562,80	312,54	230,47	190,43	167,17	125,77
7 000	656,60	364,63	268,88	222,17	195,04	146,73
8 000	750,40	416,71	307,29	253,91	222,90	167,69
9 000	844,20	468,80	345,70	285,64	250,76	188,65
10 000	938,00	520,89	384,12	317,38	278,62	209,61
15 000	1407,00	781,33	576,17	476,07	417,93	314,41
20 000	1875,99	1041,78	768,23	634,76	557,24	419,21
25 000	2344,99	1302,22	960,28	793,45	696,54	524,01
30 000	2813,99	1562,66	1152,34	952,14	835,85	628,82
35 000	3282,98	1823,11	1344,39	1110,82	975,16	733,62
40 000	3751,98	2083,55	1536,45	1269,51	1114,57	838,42
45 000	4220,98	2343,99	1728,50	1428,20	1253,77	943,22
50 000	4689,98	2604,44	1920,56	1586,89	1393,08	1048,02
60 000	5627,97	3125,32	2304,67	1904,27	1671,70	1257,63
70 000	6565,96	3646,21	2688,78	2221,64	1950,31	1467,23
80 000	7503,96	4167,10	3072,89	2539,02	2228,93	1676,83
90 000	8441,95	4687,98	3457,00	2856,40	2507,54	1886,44
100 000	9379,95	5208,87	3841,11	3173,77	2786,16	2096,04

142

Required monthly payment to refund a mortgage loan   23½%

Amount	terms of loan (in years)					
	15	20	25	30	35	40
500	9,69	9,46	9,39	9,36	9,35	9,35
1 000	19,38	18,92	18,77	18,72	18,70	18,70
2 000	38,76	37,83	37,53	37,43	37,40	37,39
3 000	58,14	56,74	56,29	56,14	56,09	56,08
4 000	77,52	75,65	75,05	74,85	74,79	74,77
5 000	96,90	94,56	93,81	93,56	93,48	93,46
6 000	116,28	113,47	112,57	112,28	112,18	112,15
7 000	135,66	132,38	131,33	130,99	130,88	130,84
8 000	155,04	151,29	150,09	149,70	149,57	149,53
9 000	174,42	170,20	168,85	168,41	168,27	168,22
10 000	193,80	189,11	187,61	187,12	186,96	186,91
15 000	290,70	283,66	281,42	280,68	280,44	280,37
20 000	387,60	378,21	375,22	374,24	373,92	373,82
25 000	484,50	472,76	469,02	467,80	467,40	467,27
30 000	581,40	567,32	562,33	561,36	560,88	560,73
35 000	678,30	661,87	656,63	654,92	654,36	654,18
40 000	775,20	756,42	750,43	748,58	747,84	747,63
45 000	872,10	850,97	844,24	842,04	841,32	841,09
50 000	969,00	945,52	938,04	935,60	934,80	934,54
60 000	1162,80	1134,63	1125,65	1122,72	1121,76	1121,45
70 000	1356,59	1323,73	1313,26	1309,84	1308,72	1308,36
80 000	1550,39	1512,83	1500,86	1496,96	1495,68	1495,26
90 000	1744,19	1701,94	1688,47	1684,08	1682,64	1682,17
100 000	1937,99	1891,04	1876,08	1871,20	1869,60	1869,08

terms of loan (in years)

Amount	1	2	3	4	5	10
500	47,01	26,16	19,33	16,00	14,07	10,64
1 000	94,02	52,32	38,65	31,99	28,13	21,28
2 000	188,04	104,63	77,30	63,98	56,25	42,55
3 000	282,06	156,95	115,95	95,96	84,37	63,82
4 000	376,08	209,26	154,60	127,95	112,49	85,10
5 000	470,10	261,58	193,24	159,94	140,62	106,37
6 000	564,12	313,89	231,89	191,92	168,74	127,64
7 000	658,14	366,21	270,54	223,91	196,86	148,92
8 000	752,16	418,52	309,19	255,90	224,98	170,19
9 000	846,18	470,83	347,84	287,88	253,10	191,46
10 000	940,19	523,15	386,48	319,87	281,23	212,73
15 000	1410,29	784,72	579,72	479,80	421,84	319,10
20 000	1880,38	1046,29	772,96	639,73	562,45	425,46
25 000	2350,48	1307,86	966,20	799,66	703,06	531,83
30 000	2820,57	1569,43	1159,44	959,60	843,67	638,19
35 000	3290,67	1831,01	1352,68	1119,53	984,28	744,56
40 000	3760,76	2092,58	1545,92	1279,46	1124,89	850,92
45 000	4230,86	2354,15	1739,16	1439,39	1265,50	957,29
50 000	4700,95	2615,72	1932,39	1599,32	1406,12	1063,65
60 000	5641,14	3138,86	2318,87	1919,19	1687,34	1276,38
70 000	6581,33	3662,01	2705,35	2239,05	1968,56	1489,11
80 000	7521,62	4185,15	3091,83	2558,92	2249,78	1701,84
90 000	8461,71	4708,29	3478,31	2878,78	2531,00	1914,57
100 000	9401,90	5231,44	3264,78	3198,64	2812,23	2127,30

144

Required monthly payment to refund a mortgage loan

24%

Amount	terms of loan (in years)					
	15	20	25	30	35	40
500	9,87	9,64	9,57	9,55	9,54	9,54
1 000	19,73	19,28	19,14	19,09	19,08	1907
2 000	39,46	38,55	38,27	38,18	38,15	38,14
3 000	59,18	57,83	57,41	57,27	57,23	57,21
4 000	78,91	77,10	76,54	76,36	76,30	76,28
5 000	98,64	96,38	95,67	95,45	95,38	95,35
6 000	118,36	115,65	114,81	114,54	114,45	114,42
7 000	138,09	134,93	133,94	133,63	133,53	133,49
8 000	157,81	154,20	153,08	152,72	152,60	152,56
9 000	177,54	173,48	172,21	171,80	171,68	171,63
10 000	197,27	192,75	191,34	190,89	190,75	190,70
15 000	295,90	289,13	287,01	286,34	286,12	286,05
20 000	394,53	385,50	382,68	381,78	381,49	381,40
25 000	493,16	481,87	478,35	477,23	476,87	476,75
30 000	591,79	578,25	574,02	572,67	572,24	572,10
35 000	690,42	674,62	669,69	668,12	667,61	667,45
40 000	789,05	771,00	765,36	763,56	762,98	762,80
45 000	887,68	867,37	861,03	859,00	858,36	858,15
50 000	986,31	963,74	956,70	954,45	953,73	953,50
60 000	1183,57	1156,49	1148,03	1145,34	1144,47	1144,19
70 000	1380,83	1349,24	1339,37	1336,23	1335,22	1334,89
80 000	1578,09	1541,99	1530,71	1527,12	1525,96	1525,59
90 000	1775,35	1734,74	1722,05	1718,00	1716,71	1716,29
100 000	1972,61	1927,48	1913,39	1908,89	1907,45	1906,99

24½% Required monthly payment to refund a mortgage loan

Amount	terms of loan (in years)					
	1	2	3	4	5	10
500	47,12	26,28	19,45	16,12	14,20	12,96
1 000	94,24	52,55	38,89	32,24	28,39	21,59
2 000	188,48	105,09	77,77	64,48	56,77	43,18
3 000	282,72	157,63	116,66	96,71	85,16	86,35
4 000	376,96	210,17	155,54	128,95	113,54	107,94
5 000	471,20	262,71	194,43	161,18	141,92	129,52
6 000	565,44	315,25	233,31	193,42	170,31	129,52
7 000	659,67	367,79	272,20	225,65	198,69	151,11
8 000	753,91	420,33	311,08	257,89	227,07	172,70
9 000	848,15	472,87	349,97	290,13	255,46	194,28
10 000	942,39	525,41	388,85	322,36	283,84	215,87
15 000	1413,58	788,11	583,28	483,54	425,76	323,80
20 000	1884,77	1050,81	777,90	644,72	567,68	431,74
25 000	2355,96	1313,51	972,13	805,90	709,60	561,26
30 000	2827,16	1576,21	1166,55	967,07	851,51	755,54
35 000	3298,35	1838,91	1360,98	1128,25	993,43	755,54
40 000	3769,54	2101,61	1555,40	1289,43	1135,35	863,47
45 000	4240,73	2364,31	1749,82	1450,61	1277,27	971,40
50 000	4711,92	2627,01	1944,25	1611,79	1419,19	1079,33
60 000	5654,31	3152,41	2333,10	1934,14	1703,02	1295,20
70 000	6596,69	3677,81	2721,95	2256,50	1986,86	1511,07
80 000	7539,08	4203,21	3110,79	2578,86	2270,70	1726,93
90 000	8481,46	4728,61	3499,64	2901,21	2554,53	1942,80
100 000	9423,84	5254,01	3888,49	3223,57	2838,37	2158,66

Required monthly payment to refund a mortgage loan   24½%

Amount	terms of loan (in years)					
	15	20	25	30	35	40
500	10,04	9,82	9,76	9,74	9,73	9,73
1 000	20,08	19,64	19,51	19,47	19,46	19,45
2 000	40,15	39,28	39,02	38,94	38,91	38,90
3 000	60,22	58,92	58,53	58,40	58,36	58,35
4 000	80,30	78,56	78,03	77,87	77,81	77,80
5 000	100,37	98,20	97,54	97,33	97,27	97,25
6 000	120,44	117,84	117,05	116,80	116,72	116,69
7 000	140,52	137,48	136,55	136,26	135,17	136,14
8 000	160,59	157,12	156,06	155,73	155,62	155,59
9 000	180,66	176,76	175,57	175,19	175,08	175,04
10 000	200,74	196,40	195,07	194,66	194,53	194,59
15 000	301,10	294,60	292,61	291,98	291,79	291,73
20 000	401,47	392,79	390,14	389,31	389,05	388,97
25 000	501,83	490,99	487,67	486,64	486,31	486,21
30 000	602,20	589,19	585,21	583,96	583,57	583,45
35 000	702,56	687,38	682,74	681,29	680,84	680,69
40 000	802,93	785,58	780,27	778,62	778,10	777,93
45 000	903,29	883,78	877,81	875,94	875,36	875,18
50 000	1003,66	981,98	975,34	973,27	972,62	972,42
60 000	1204,39	1178,37	1170,41	1167,42	1167,14	1166,90
70 000	1405,12	1374,76	1365,48	1362,58	1361,67	1361,38
80 000	1605,85	1571,16	1560,54	1557,23	1556,19	1555,86
90 000	1806,58	1767,55	1755,61	1751,88	1750,71	1750,35
100 000	2007,31	1963,95	1950,68	1946,54	1945,24	1944,83

	terms of loan (in years)					
Amount	1	2	3	4	5	10
500	47,23	26,39	19,57	16,25	14,33	10,96
1 000	94,46	52,77	39,13	32,49	28,65	21,91
2 000	188,92	105,54	78,25	64,98	57,30	43,81
3 000	283,38	158,30	117,37	97,46	85,94	65,71
4 000	377,84	211,07	156,49	129,95	114,59	87,61
5 000	472,29	263,84	195,62	162,43	143,23	109,51
6 000	566,75	316,60	234,74	194,92	171,88	131,41
7 000	661,21	369,37	273,86	227,40	200,53	153,31
8 000	755,67	422,13	312,98	259,89	229,17	175,22
9 000	850,12	474,90	352,11	292,37	257,82	197,12
10 000	944,58	527,67	391,23	324,86	286,46	219,02
15 000	1416,87	791,50	586,84	487,29	429,69	328,53
20 000	1889,16	1055,33	782,45	649,71	572,92	438,03
25 000	2361,45	1319,16	978,06	812,14	716,15	547,54
30 000	2833,74	1582,99	1173,67	974,57	859,38	657,05
35 000	3306,02	1846,82	1369,29	1137,00	1002,61	766,55
40 000	3778,31	2110,65	1564,90	1299,42	1145,84	876,06
45 000	4250,60	2374,48	1760,51	1461,85	1289,07	985,57
50 000	4722,89	2638,31	1956,12	1624,28	1432,30	1095,07
60 000	5667,27	3165,97	2347,34	1949,13	1719,75	1314,09
70 000	6612,04	3693,63	2738,57	2273,99	2005,21	1533,10
80 000	7556,62	4221,29	3129,79	2598,84	2291,67	1752,11
90 000	8501,20	4748,95	3521,01	2923,70	2578,13	1971,13
100 000	9445,77	5276,61	3912,24	3248,55	2864,59	2190,14

Required monthly payment to refund a mortgage loan

25%

terms of loan (in years)

Amount	15	20	25	30	35	40
500	10,22	10,01	9,94	9,93	9,92	9,92
1 000	20,43	20,01	19,88	19,85	19,83	19,83
2 000	40,85	40,01	39,76	39,69	39,66	39,66
3 000	61,27	60,02	59,64	59,53	59,49	59,48
4 000	81,69	80,02	79,52	79,37	79,32	79,31
5 000	102,11	100,03	99,40	99,21	99,15	99,14
6 000	122,53	120,03	119,28	119,05	118,98	118,96
7 000	142,95	140,04	139,16	138,89	138,81	138,79
8 000	163,37	160,04	159,04	158,74	158,64	158,61
9 000	183,79	180,04	178,92	178,58	178,47	178,44
10 000	204,21	200,05	198,80	198,42	198,30	198,27
15 000	306,32	300,07	298,20	297,63	297,45	297,40
20 000	408,42	400,09	397,59	396,83	396,60	396,53
25 000	510,52	500,11	496,99	496,04	495,75	495,66
30 000	612,63	600,14	596,39	595,25	594,89	594,99
35 000	714,73	700,16	695,79	694,45	694,04	693,92
40 000	816,84	800,18	795,18	793,66	793,19	793,05
45 000	918,94	900,20	894,58	892,87	892,34	892,18
50 000	1021,54	1000,22	993,98	992,07	991,49	991,31
60 000	1225,25	1200,27	1192,77	1190,49	1189,78	1189,57
70 000	1429,46	1400,31	1391,57	1388,90	1388,68	1387,53
80 000	1633,67	1600,35	1590,36	1587,31	1586,38	1586,09
90 000	1837,88	1800,40	1789,16	1785,73	1784,67	1784,35
100 000	2042,08	2000,44	1987,95	1984,14	1982,97	1982,61

Required monthly payment to refund a mortgage loan

Amount	terms of loan (in years)					
	1	2	3	4	5	10
500	47,45	26,61	19,80	16,50	14,59	11,27
1 000	94,90	53,22	39,60	32,99	29,18	22,54
2 000	189,80	106,44	79,20	65,98	58,35	45,07
3 000	284,69	159,66	118,80	98,97	87,52	67,61
4 000	379,59	212,88	158,40	131,95	116,69	90,14
5 000	474,48	266,10	198,00	164,94	145,87	112,68
6 000	569,38	319,31	237,59	197,93	175,04	135,21
7 000	664,28	372,53	277,19	230,91	204,21	157,74
8 000	759,17	425,75	316,79	263,90	233,38	180,28
9 000	854,07	478,97	356,39	296,89	262,56	202,81
10 000	948,96	532,19	395,99	329,87	291,73	225,35
15 000	1423,44	798,28	593,98	494,81	437,59	338,02
20 000	1897,92	1064,37	791,97	659,74	583,45	450,69
25 000	2372,40	1330,46	989,96	824,67	729,31	563,36
30 000	2846,88	1596,55	1187,95	989,61	875,17	676,03
35 000	3321,36	1862,64	1385,94	1154,54	1021,04	788,70
40 000	3795,84	2128,73	1583,93	1319,48	1166,90	901,37
45 000	4270,32	2394,82	1781,93	1484,41	1312,76	1014,04
50 000	4744,80	2660,91	1979,92	1649,34	1458,62	1126,71
60 000	5693,76	3193,10	2375,90	1979,21	1750,34	1352,05
70 000	6642,71	3725,28	2771,88	2309,08	2042,07	1577,39
80 000	7591,67	4257,46	3167,86	2638,95	2333,79	1802,73
90 000	8540,63	4789,64	3563,85	2968,81	2625,51	2028,07
100 000	9489,59	5321,82	3959,83	3298,68	2917,23	2253,41

Required monthly payment to refund a mortgage loan — 26%

Amount	terms of loan (in years)					
	15	20	25	30	35	40
500	10,56	10,37	10,32	10,30	10,30	10,29
1 000	21,12	20,74	20,63	20,60	20,59	20,58
2 000	42,24	41,47	41,25	41,19	41,17	41,16
3 000	63,36	62,21	61,88	61,78	61,75	61,74
4 000	84,48	82,94	82,50	82,37	82,33	82,32
5 000	105,60	103,68	103,13	102,96	102,92	102,90
6 000	126,72	124,41	123,75	123,56	123,50	123,48
7 000	147,83	145,15	144,37	144,15	144,08	144,06
8 000	168,95	165,88	165,00	164,74	164,66	164,64
9 000	190,07	186,62	185,62	185,33	185,25	185,22
10 000	211,19	207,35	206,25	205,92	205,83	205,80
15 000	316,78	311,02	309,37	308,88	308,74	308,70
20 000	422,37	414,70	412,49	411,84	411,65	411,60
25 000	527,96	518,37	515,61	514,80	514,57	514,50
30 000	633,56	622,04	618,73	617,76	617,48	617,39
35 000	739,15	725,72	721,85	720,72	720,39	720,29
40 000	844,74	829,39	824,97	823,68	823,30	823,19
45 000	950,33	933,06	928,09	926,64	926,21	926,09
50 000	1055,92	1036,74	1031,22	1029,60	1029,13	1028,99
60 000	1267,11	1244,08	1237,46	1235,52	1234,95	1234,78
70 000	1478,29	1451,43	1443,70	1441,44	1440,77	1440,58
80 000	1689,47	1658,77	1649,94	1647,36	1646,60	1646,38
90 000	1900,66	1866,12	1856,18	1853,28	1852,42	1852,17
100 000	2111,84	2073,47	2062,43	2059,20	2058,25	2057,97

Required monthly payment to refund a mortgage loan

terms of loan (in years)

Amount	1	2	3	4	5	10
500	47,67	26,84	20,04	16,75	14,86	11,59
1 000	95,34	53,68	40,08	33,50	29,71	23,18
2 000	190,67	107,35	80,16	66,99	59,41	46,35
3 000	286,01	161,02	120,23	100,48	89,11	69,52
4 000	381,34	214,69	160,31	133,97	118,81	92,69
5 000	476,67	268,36	200,38	167,46	148,51	115,86
6 000	572,01	322,03	240,46	200,95	178,21	139,03
7 000	667,34	375,70	280,53	234,44	207,92	162,20
8 000	762,67	429,37	320,61	267,93	237,62	185,37
9 000	858,01	483,04	360,68	301,42	267,32	208,54
10 000	953,34	536,71	400,76	334,91	297,02	231,71
15 000	1430,01	805,07	601,14	502,36	445,53	347,56
20 000	1906,67	1073,42	801,52	669,81	594,04	463,42
25 000	2383,34	1341,78	1001,89	837,26	742,54	579,27
30 000	2860,01	1610,13	1202,27	1004,71	891,05	695,12
35 000	3336,68	1878,48	1402,65	1172,16	1039,56	810,98
40 000	3813,34	2146,84	1603,03	1339,61	1188,07	926,83
45 000	4290,01	2415,19	1803,40	1507,06	1336,58	1042,68
50 000	4766,68	2683,55	2003,78	1674,52	1485,08	1158,53
60 000	5720,01	3220,26	2404,54	2009,42	1782,10	1390,24
70 000	6673,35	3756,96	2805,29	2344,32	2079,11	1621,95
80 000	7626,68	4293,67	3206,05	2679,22	2376,13	1853,65
90 000	8580,02	4830,38	3606,80	3014,12	2673,15	2085,36
100 000	9533,35	5367,09	4007,56	3349,03	2970,16	2317,06

Required monthly payment to refund a mortgage loan

27%

Amount	terms of loan (in years)					
	15	20	25	30	35	40
500	10,91	10,74	10,69	10,68	10,67	10,67
1 000	21,82	21,47	21,37	21,35	21,34	21,34
2 000	43,64	42,94	42,74	42,69	42,67	42,67
3 000	65,46	64,40	64,11	64,03	64,00	64,00
4 000	87,28	85,87	85,48	85,37	85,34	85,33
5 000	109,10	107,33	106,84	106,71	106,67	106,66
6 000	130,91	128,80	128,21	128,05	128,00	127,99
7 000	152,73	150,26	149,58	149,39	149,33	149,32
8 000	174,55	171,73	170,95	170,73	170,67	170,65
9 000	196,37	193,19	192,31	192,07	192,00	191,98
10 000	218,19	214,66	213,68	213,41	213,33	213,31
15 000	327,28	321,98	320,52	320,11	320,00	319,96
20 000	436,37	429,31	427,36	426,81	426,66	426,62
25 000	545,46	536,64	534,20	533,52	533,32	533,27
30 000	654,55	643,96	641,04	640,22	639,99	639,92
35 000	763,65	751,29	747,88	746,92	746,65	746,58
40 000	872,74	858,61	854,71	853,62	853,31	853,23
45 000	981,83	965,94	961,55	960,32	959,98	959,88
50 000	1090,92	1073,27	1068,39	1067,03	1066,64	1066,53
60 000	1309,10	1287,92	1282,07	1280,43	1279,97	1279,84
70 000	1527,29	1502,57	1495,75	1493,83	1493,30	1493,15
80 000	1745,47	1717,22	1709,42	1707,24	1706,62	1706,45
90 000	1963,65	1931,88	1923,10	1920,64	1919,95	1919,76
100 000	2181,84	2146,53	2136,78	2134,05	2133,28	2133,06

28% Required monthly payment to refund a mortgage loan

terms of loan (in years)

Amount	1	2	3	4	5	10
500	47,89	27,07	20,28	17,00	15,12	11,91
1 000	95,78	54,13	40,56	34,00	30,24	23,82
2 000	191,55	108,25	81,11	68,00	60,47	47,63
3 000	287,32	162,38	121,67	101,99	90,71	71,44
4 000	383,09	216,50	162,22	135,99	120,94	95,25
5 000	478,86	270,62	202,78	169,98	151,17	119,06
6 000	574,63	324,75	243,33	203,98	181,41	142,87
7 000	670,40	378,87	283,88	237,98	211,64	166,68
8 000	766,17	433,00	324,44	271,97	241,87	190,49
9 000	861,94	487,12	364,99	305,97	272,11	214,30
10 000	957,11	541,24	405,55	339,96	302,34	238,11
15 000	1436,56	811,86	608,32	509,94	453,51	357,17
20 000	1915,42	1082,48	811,09	679,92	604,68	476,22
25 000	2394,27	1353,10	1013,86	849,90	755,84	595,27
30 000	2873,12	1623,72	1216,63	1019,88	907,01	714,33
35 000	3351,98	1894,34	1419,40	1189,86	1058,18	833,38
40 000	3830,83	2164,96	1622,17	1359,84	1209,35	952,43
45 000	4309,68	2435,58	1824,94	1529,81	1360,51	1071,49
50 000	4788,54	2706,20	2027,71	1699,79	1511,68	1190,54
60 000	5746,24	3247,44	2433,26	2039,75	1814,02	1428,65
70 000	6703,95	3788,68	2838,80	2379,71	2116,35	1666,76
80 000	7661,65	4329,92	3244,34	2719,67	2418,69	1904,86
90 000	8619,36	4871,16	3649,88	3059,62	2721,02	2142,97
100 000	9577,07	5412,40	4055,42	3399,58	3023,36	2381,08

Required monthly payment to refund a mortgage loan   28%

terms of loan (in years)

Amount	15	20	25	30	35	40
500	11,27	11,10	11,06	11,05	11,05	11,04
1 000	22,53	22,20	22,11	22,09	22,09	22,08
2 000	45,05	44,40	44,22	44,18	44,17	44,16
3 000	67,57	66,59	66,33	66,27	66,25	66,24
4 000	90,09	88,79	88,44	88,35	88,33	88,32
5 000	112,61	110,98	110,55	110,44	110,41	110,40
6 000	135,13	133,18	132,66	132,53	132,49	132,48
7 000	157,65	155,38	154,77	154,61	154,57	154,56
8 000	180,17	177,57	176,88	176,70	176,65	176,64
9 000	202,69	199,77	198,99	198,79	198,73	198,71
10 000	225,21	221,96	221,10	220,87	220,81	220,79
15 000	337,81	332,94	331,65	331,31	331,21	331,19
20 000	450,41	443,92	442,20	441,74	441,62	441,58
25 000	563,01	554,90	552,75	552,17	552,02	551,98
30 000	675,61	665,88	663,30	662,61	662,42	662,37
35 000	788,21	776,86	773,85	773,04	772,82	772,76
40 000	900,81	887,83	884,40	883,47	883,23	883,16
45 000	1013,42	998,81	994,95	993,91	993,63	993,55
50 000	1126,02	1109,79	1105,50	1104,34	1104,03	1103,95
60 000	1351,22	1331,75	1326,59	1325,21	1324,84	1324,74
70 000	1576,42	1553,71	1547,69	1546,08	1545,64	1545,52
80 000	1801,62	1775,66	1768,79	1766,94	1766,45	1766,31
90 000	2026,83	1997,62	1989,89	1987,81	1987,25	1987,10
100 000	2252,03	2219,58	2210,99	2208,68	2208,06	2207,89

Required monthly payment to refund a mortgage loan

terms of loan (in years)

Amount	1	2	3	4	5	10
500	48,11	27,29	20,52	17,26	15,39	12,23
1 000	96,21	54,58	41,04	34,51	30,77	24,46
2 000	192,42	109,16	82,07	69,01	61,54	48,91
3 000	288,63	163,74	123,11	103,51	92,31	73,37
4 000	384,83	218,32	164,14	138,02	123,08	97,82
5 000	481.04	272,89	205,18	172,52	153,85	122,28
6 000	577,25	327,47	246,21	207,02	184,61	146,73
7 000	673,46	382,05	287,24	241,53	215,38	171,18
8 000	769,66	436,63	328,28	276,03	246,15	195,64
9 000	865,87	491,20	369,31	310,53	276,92	220,09
10 000	962,08	545,78	410,35	345,04	307,69	244,55
15 000	1443,11	818,67	615,52	517,55	461,53	366,82
20 000	1924,15	1091,56	820,69	690,07	615,37	489,09
25 000	2405,19	1364,44	1025,86	862,59	769,21	611,36
30 000	2886,22	1637,33	1231,03	1035,10	923,05	733,63
35 000	3367,26	1910,22	1436,20	1207,62	1076,89	855,90
40 000	3848,29	2183,11	1641,37	1380,14	1230,73	978,17
45 000	4329,33	2455,99	1846,54	1552,65	1384,57	1100,44
50 000	4810,37	2728,88	2051,71	1725,17	1538,41	1222,72
60 000	5772,44	3274,66	2462,05	2070,20	1846,09	1467,26
70 000	6734,51	3820,43	2872,39	2415,24	2153,77	1711,80
80 000	7696,58	4366,21	3282,73	2760,27	2461,46	1956,34
90 000	8658,65	4911,98	3693,07	3105,30	2769,14	2200,88
100 000	9620,73	5457,76	4103,41	3450,34	3076,82	2445,43

Required monthly payment to refund a mortgage loan **29%**

Amount	terms of loan (in years)					
	15	20	25	30	35	40
500	11,62	11,47	11,43	11,42	11,42	11,42
1 000	23,23	22,93	22,86	22,84	22,83	22,83
2 000	46,45	45,86	45,71	45,67	45,66	45,65
3 000	69,68	68,78	68,56	68,50	68,48	68,48
4 000	92,90	91,71	91,41	91,33	91,31	91,30
5 000	116,12	114,63	114,26	114,16	114,13	114,13
6 000	139,35	137,56	137,11	136,99	136,96	136,95
7 000	162,57	160,49	159,96	159,82	159,79	159,78
8 000	185,79	183,41	182,81	182,65	182,61	182,60
9 000	209,02	206,34	205,66	205,48	205,44	205,43
10 000	232,24	229,26	228,51	228,31	228,26	228,25
15 000	348,36	343,89	342,76	342,47	342,39	342,37
20 000	464,48	458,52	457,01	456,62	456,52	456,49
25 000	580,60	573,15	571,26	570,77	570,65	570,62
30 000	696,72	687,78	685,51	684,93	684,78	684,74
35 000	812,84	802,41	799,76	799,08	798,91	798,86
40 000	928,95	917,04	914,01	913,24	913,03	912,98
45 000	1045,07	1031,67	1028,26	1027,39	1027,16	1027,11
50 000	1161,19	1146,30	1142,52	1141,54	1141,29	1141,23
60 000	1393,43	1375,56	1371,02	1369,85	1369,55	1369,47
70 000	1625,67	1604,82	1599,52	1598,16	1597,81	1597,72
80 000	1857,90	1834,08	1828,02	1826,47	1826,06	1825,96
90 000	2090,14	2063,33	2056,52	2054,77	2054,32	2054,21
100 000	2322,38	2292,59	2285,03	2283,08	2282,58	2082,45

30% Required monthly payment to refund a mortgage loan

terms of loan (in years)

Amount	1	2	3	4	5	10
500	48,33	27,52	20,76	17,51	15,66	12,56
1 000	96,65	55,04	41,52	35,02	31,31	25,11
2 000	193,29	110,07	83,04	70,03	62,62	50,21
3 000	289,93	165,10	124,55	105,04	93,92	75,31
4 000	386,58	220,13	166,07	140,06	125,23	100,41
5 000	483,22	275,16	207,58	175,07	156,53	125,51
6 000	579,86	330,19	249,10	210,08	187,84	150,61
7 000	676,51	385,23	290,61	245,09	219,14	175,71
8 000	773,15	440,26	332,13	280,11	250,45	200,81
9 000	869,79	495,29	373,64	315,12	281,75	225,91
10 000	966,44	550,32	415,16	350,13	313,06	251,01
15 000	1449,65	825,48	622,73	525,20	469,58	376,52
20 000	1932,87	1100,64	830,31	700,26	626,11	502,02
25 000	2416,09	1375,79	1037,89	875,33	782,64	627,52
30 000	2899,30	1650,95	1245,46	1050,39	939,16	753,03
35 000	3382,52	1926,11	1453,04	1225,45	1095,69	878,53
40 000	3865,74	2201,27	1660,62	1400,52	1252,21	1004,03
45 000	4348,95	2476,42	1868,19	1575,58	1408,74	1129,54
50 000	4832,17	2751,58	2075,77	1750,65	1565,27	1255,04
60 000	5798,60	3301,90	2490,92	2100,77	1878,32	1506,05
70 000	6765,03	3852,21	2906,07	2450,90	2191,37	1757,06
80 000	7731,47	4402,53	3321,23	2801,03	2504,42	2008,06
90 000	8697,90	4952,84	3736,38	3151,16	2817,48	2259,07
100 000	9664,33	5503,16	4151,53	3501,29	3130,53	2510,08

Required monthly payment to refund a mortgage loan

30%

Amount	terms of loan (in years)					
	15	20	25	30	35	40
500	11,97	11,83	11,80	11,79	11,79	11,79
1 000	23,93	23,66	23,59	23,58	23,57	23,57
2 000	47,86	47,32	47,18	47,15	47,14	47,14
3 000	71,79	70,97	70,77	70,72	70,71	70,71
4 000	95,72	94,63	94,36	94,29	94,28	94,27
5 000	119,65	118,28	117,95	117,87	117,85	117,84
6 000	143,58	141,94	141,54	141,44	141,42	141,41
7 000	167,50	165,59	165,13	165,01	164,98	164,98
8 000	191,43	189,25	188,72	188,58	188,55	188,54
9 000	215,36	212,90	212,30	212,16	212,12	212,11
10 000	239,29	236,56	235,89	235,73	235,69	235,68
15 000	358,93	354,84	353,84	353,59	353,53	353,52
20 000	478,57	473,11	471,78	471,45	471,37	471,35
25 000	598,22	591,39	589,73	589,32	589,21	589,19
30 000	717,86	709,67	707,67	707,18	707,06	707,03
35 000	837,50	827,94	825,61	825,04	824,90	824,86
40 000	957,14	946,22	943,56	942,90	942,74	942,70
45 000	1076,79	1064,50	1061,50	1060,76	1060,58	1060,54
50 000	1196,43	1182,77	1179,45	1178,63	1178,42	1178,37
60 000	1435,71	1419,33	1415,33	1414,35	1414,11	1414,05
70 000	1675,00	1655,88	1651,22	1650,08	1649,79	1649,72
80 000	1914,28	1892,43	1887,11	1885,80	1885,48	1885,40
90 000	2153,57	2128,99	2123,00	2121,52	2121,16	2121,07
100 000	2392,85	2365,54	2358,89	2357,25	2356,84	2356,74

Achevé d'imprimé
en janvier 1993 sur les presses
de l'Imprimerie d'Arthabaska Inc.
Arthabaska, Qué.